DETACHMENT

T0204376

DETACHMENT

AN ADOPTION MEMOIR

MAURICE MIERAU

Freehand Books gratefully acknowledges the support of the Canada Council for the Arts for its publishing program. ¶ Freehand Books, an imprint of Broadview Press Inc., acknowledges the financial support for its publishing program provided by the Government of Canada through the Canada Book Fund.

 Canada Council   Conseil des Arts
for the Arts   du Canada   Government

Freehand Books
515 – 815 1st Street SW Calgary, Alberta T2P 1N3
www.freehand-books.com

Book orders: LitDistCo
100 Armstrong Avenue Georgetown, Ontario L7G 5S4
Telephone: 1-800-591-6250 Fax: 1-800-591-6251
orders@litdistco.ca
www.litdistco.ca

Library and Archives Canada Cataloguing in Publication

Mierau, Maurice, 1962–, author
Detachment : an adoption memoir / Maurice Mierau.

Issued in print and electronic formats.
ISBN 978-1-55481-206-6 (pbk.).
ISBN 978-1-4604-0455-3 (epub).
ISBN 978-1-77048-492-4 (pdf).

1. Mierau, Maurice, 1962–. 2. Mierau, Maurice, 1962– — Family.
3. Adoptive parents — Canada — Biography. 4. Adopted children — Ukraine — Biography. 5. Fathers and sons — Canada — Biography. I. Title.

PS8576.I2858Z464 2014   C811'.54   C2014-902423-1
                                                  C2014-902424-X

Edited by Barbara Scott
Book design and illustration by Natalie Olsen, Kisscut Design
Author photo by Merrell-Ann Phare

Printed on FSC recycled paper and bound in Canada

to my sons
Bohdan, Peter, and Jeremy
with love

"... a child's post-traumatic stress symptoms, including explosive and uncontrolled emotions, are significantly reduced when he hears the parent tell the story of the traumatic events, specifically acknowledging the child's feelings and perceptions about them."

—**PATTY COGEN**, *Parenting Your Internationally Adopted Child*

CONTENTS

SHRINKING

The psychologist's office was above a bank in a Winnipeg strip mall. The psychologist was blonde and a bit puffy around the eyes, wearing Birkenstocks and no makeup. She had my ex-wife's first name.

I sat on a couch opposite her. Winter light poured into the large room from windows facing the street and I wished it were dark. She leaned toward me across the coffee table.

"Why don't you tell me why you're here?"

I'd spoken to her on the phone, and wasn't sure why she wanted me to repeat myself. I thought of my wife, Betsy, another over-communicator. She'd begged me to seek help for three years. She'd also started to swear a lot since we watched *The Sopranos* together.

"I have problems in my marriage, marital problems I guess."

"You're not sure?" She smiled.

"I don't really have any huge problem," I said. "I haven't cheated on my wife or had panic attacks. She yells and accuses me of being like my dad." The therapist stopped smiling. Maybe she didn't get the *Sopranos* reference.

"Are you nervous?"

"No." I realized that I'd been touching my glasses and tapping the back of my head like a fidgeting child.

"Why are you here, Maurice?"

A glass of water stood in front of me and I picked it up now, drinking fast. I felt vaguely disgusted with myself.

"Betsy is ready to leave and take the kids with her. I've already lost one kid in a breakup, and — I won't do it again."

"Why does Betsy accuse you of being like your dad?"

"She says I refuse to talk about my feelings. She says I change the subject when it gets difficult. She calls me *Eric*, and then cuts off the conversation."

"Eric is your father?"

"That's right." I took off my glasses and rubbed my eyes, thinking of my last fight with Betsy. I told her to be logical and she told me to fuck off when I followed her around the house apologizing.

"Is she right about what you do in these arguments?"

"Of course." In the silence that followed I heard the traffic sounds from the street.

"What feelings do you refuse to discuss with her?"

"Mostly anger." A heavier silence now, as if the room and the plants and the sunlight expected more from me. I held my breath while she wrote on her pad.

"What are you angry about?" She stopped her pen and I exhaled.

"I wasted so many years. It was stupid. I'm a full-time writer now, but I should have started much sooner." I paused again, cleared my throat.

"Why didn't you start sooner?"

"My first wife was in graduate school and I'd agreed to pay the bills while she finished. There were a lot of jobs I couldn't stand, mostly selling things, computers." I took another drink of the water. "I paid the bills and lost a decade of my life."

"You could have made other choices, right?"

"Yes, that's part of what pisses me off. It made me a shitty father to my oldest son, Jeremy. Last year I think he flunked some of his university courses and lied to me about the grades."

"Why do you think you weren't a good father to Jeremy?"

"Because I was preoccupied with myself and my own problems. And so I worry that I'll fuck things up with Peter and Bohdan the same way I have with Jeremy."

"Peter and Bohdan are your younger sons?"

"Yes, Betsy and I adopted them in Ukraine when Peter was five and Bohdan was three. Four years ago, in 2005."

"And you said on the phone that Peter has seen a therapist as well?"

"He was diagnosed with attachment disorder after his second year with us. The first year went great. But then last year he ran away from home, he's been stealing things, and now he shouts at me in public." When Peter ran away I'd found him in a nearby alley, his face twisting with anger. He refused to come with me, and I had to half-carry, half-drag him home. He struggled so much that for a week afterward my body felt like it had been pounded by a meat tenderizer.

"How do you feel about that?"

"Embarrassed. Angry. In need of a drink." I didn't say it out loud but I worried that he'd run again. God knows I often wanted to run away myself. "Peter remembers more than Bohdan, and maybe that's the problem. The boys' mother abandoned them with a boyfriend, and then she failed to show up in court, lost her parental rights. Bohdan doesn't remember the orphanage at all, but he has unbelievable temper tantrums sometimes." I paused while the therapist wrote in tight cursive on her pad.

"The night Peter ran, after he calmed down, we told him what his birth parents had done. He said, 'How can I trust anyone again?' He sobbed because he had no pictures of his parents. He wanted to know what his father's knees looked like."

I took a ragged breath. "All stories are about betrayal," I said, because I did not want to start crying. In the orphanage they'd been separated into different wings of the institution because of their age difference; they only saw each other on major religious holidays.

"What does Peter remember from the orphanage?" the psychologist asked.

"He remembers an ambulance, lights and sirens, a few other children his age. Someone gave him a backpack. They drove for a long time and he was scared. He went from the baby orphanage, where he'd lived for about a year, to the orphanage for older children out in the country. No one explained to Peter where he was going, or if he would ever see his younger brother again. Peter had no chance to say goodbye to Bohdan, he remembers that.

"He knows how the siren sounded on that drive. He was four. Now he knows how many times the crosswalk blinks on the way to school. Bohdan has an excellent memory too. He remembers every dessert he ever had from the age of three."

My throat constricted, stains appeared on my glasses, and my nose ran. The therapist handed me the box of tissues. I took two, three of them, and blew my nose.

"That's the hour," she said. "Should we make another appointment now?"

"I don't know. Have we achieved anything?"

"I think we just started."

———

December was always a hard time for Peter. It was the month his mother abandoned him. A trauma-versary, they called this on the adoptive-parent blogs that Betsy read. I didn't like the

Christmas season either although my reasons differed from Peter's. On my last visit of 2009 to the psychologist's office, the only sign of the holidays was a miniature artificial tree in the waiting room.

The psychologist asked why we adopted in Ukraine. I explained that we knew some people who adopted kids there, and also my father and his family came from Ukraine.

"But growing up, I didn't hear much about his past."

"Why was that?"

"Dad had a terrible childhood. You could say he never had one." I paused, choking up again, annoyed with myself for losing control.

"What happened to him?"

"His family fled with the German army from Soviet Ukraine in 1943."

"Why was he fleeing with the Germans?"

"Dad's family were Mennonite people, German-speaking, and his mother was a widow. She needed protection. She got together with a German agricultural officer, and he took them west through the Soviet Union to Poland, all the way to Germany."

"What has your father told you about what that trip was like?"

"Almost nothing."

"Has he told you anything about his childhood?"

"Very little. He was an orphan by the time he was ten, and Lil, his older sister, raised him. I know that his earliest memory is seeing a group of Jewish families shot into a ditch. He told me that last year."

"What was the occasion?"

"I just asked him. The boys and I were visiting Mom and Dad in Edmonton. It was spring break, Betsy was working. We talked about the earliest things Peter remembers, which led to the subject of what Dad's earliest memory was."

"How did his parents die?"

"His father was shot during Stalin's Great Terror, in 1938. His mother died of a hospital infection in Germany three years after the war. Most of what I know comes from Dad's sister Lil."

"Have you talked to your dad about what else he remembers?"

"Yes. He remembers fragments: being on the back of a truck with his mom and Lil, driving through burning villages: that was in Ukraine. My dad remembers the Soviet soldiers coming onto his stepfather's estate in Germany, and he can describe the destruction of the estate in detail. But what happened to his mother that day is a blank for him, even though he was right there and Lil remembers it all." I can feel lunch sloshing up into my throat.

"What do you make of that?"

"He doesn't want this shit on his mind."

She didn't react. "Are you angry at him?"

"At my dad?"

She nodded.

"I was, maybe I still am."

"Why?"

"Oh Christ." By the time I turned seventeen and left home for college, we had lived at thirty-four different addresses. And from then on it was always my job to call home; Dad called only on birthdays. "Through my childhood, my father kept changing jobs. We travelled a lot. I was born in the US and we lived in Nigeria during the civil war in the late '60s, in Jamaica in the '70s."

For a moment I was five years old, waking up sweaty in white sheets and under mosquito netting, afraid, and calling my mom. Dad was off somewhere, helping missionaries translate the Bible. Mom came at a run because she was scared that I had a malarial fever and there was no one to drive me to the hospital; she didn't drive.

In 2004, when I'd tried writing essays about my childhood, my father lent me his and my mother's diaries from the years we lived in Africa. He and my mother wanted to help. Dad let these intimate documents speak for him. By that time my mother had started showing early signs of dementia, and even though she used to talk like a Russian novel, now she hardly spoke.

"Do you wish your childhood had been more stable?"

"Yes, of course. Although in some ways I had a happy childhood." In Jamaica I made Lego cars with Dad and we spent hours racing them on the long patio at the front of our house. He made sandcastles with me and my sister at the beach. I went to the library and lived in the books I found: *Treasure Island, David Copperfield,* books about Harry Houdini and the American Civil War. Every time we moved, my sister, who was two years younger than me, wept about her lost friends. I didn't cry because by the age of five I knew that friendships never lasted long, and besides, every town had a new library with more books to read. My life was an adventure, I told myself then, and I did not feel lonely.

"Can we talk about why I'm here? About my marriage?"

"Betsy still won't come and see me, either with you or on her own, will she?" she asked, as if to emphasize my solitary presence.

I shrugged.

"You're very angry," she said.

How perceptive, I thought.

Spring is Winnipeg's worst season, the time of dirt and dog shit and fear of the rivers flooding, sewage in your basement. On a dim, cold day I walked through the long hall to the psychologist's office for my third monthly session after the first ones in 2009. In the reception area where no receptionist worked, I waited for a few minutes. Then the therapist called me in. For the last few meetings she had sat a car-length away from me, behind an oak desk.

"How have things been with your family, Maurice?"

"Not much has changed. Every weekend Betsy makes these big lists of chores and kids' activities and groceries and what-have-you. She's perfectly organized."

"What would you rather do on the weekend?"

"I don't know — scream like a demented blues singer." I laughed without humour. "I'm just tired of the schedule, and how she always wants to control everything, all her preferences that she accuses me of forgetting, all her Ideas about Everything."

"In our first meeting you said Betsy had threatened to leave you. Why did she do that?"

"She says I'm not tuned into her or the kids. But she tunes me out too. She used to be so in love with me." My voice sounded whiny and I stopped to look at my watch, infuriated at what all this pointless talk would cost, and how underemployed writers have to depend on their partner's insurance.

"How do you know she's not in love with you now?"

"She says it's not about love. Which is true, obviously."

"Why are you so angry at her?"

"I don't know. Maybe I'm just scared." This was not my first time with a shrink. I knew my lines in the script. She wanted me to have an Oprah moment, to meet Jesus on Therapy Street. Some lines from Fernando Pessoa spoke to me in my head:

> *The poet is a faker*
> *Who's so good at his act*
> *He even fakes the pain*
> *Of pain he feels in fact.*

A litany of my past fakeries crashed over me: my fake response to an altar call in my teens, my fake hug when dispatching a former girlfriend, my fake good manners when I just wanted to tell everybody to fuck off. Even for the shrink I could only pander to expectations by faking my distinct form of pain: *fear*.

"What are you scared of?"

"I'm scared of losing everything, just like I did with Jeremy. I paid bills like crazy and hardly had any custody." What a lazy summary. I took my glasses off and rubbed them on my shirttail as if completing a major task: another dishonest gesture, anything to avoid the ugly details of Jeremy's teenage years, the cheques I wrote to his mother, the scripted pep-talks I gave him about his school work, my own self-pity.

"Is Betsy right that you're not tuned in?"

"Sure. Often I feel detached, like I'm watching from the outside. Someone will say something at dinner, or something upsetting or important happens to the boys at school, and I don't even remember."

"Does that remind you of your father?"

"Yes, it reminds me of Dad," I said after some silence, rubbing my nose nervously.

"How so?"

"I have some of the same problems he does."

"And what are those?"

"Changing the scenery, running away from what's difficult." My volume and pitch had been rising.

"What's difficult, Maurice?"

"Paying attention." I paused, trying to put my difficulty into words. "I'm never completely *with* my sons or Betsy. Often I'm thinking about work. I want to write a book about my dad's childhood and Peter's and Bohdan's."

"So you're writing a book about people you ignore. How come?"

It could have been Betsy's question, although she'd never put it to me so bluntly. I was furious, beyond words. I knew Betsy resented my obsession with the past, when she and the boys needed me so much in the present.

"Really I don't want to talk about the book." My voice sounded mild.

"How would paying attention to your kids, how would that help you?"

"This is my last chance to be their father. They need that, and so do I." My voice cracked and I looked down at my watch to avoid eye contact. I needed to get away from her bright room.

ADOPTION

I

Betsy and I arrived in Kyiv on January 31, 2005. Nikolai, the adoption agency's main operative, met us in the reception area of the Boryspil Airport. Nikolai had sent me a picture of himself by email, after I wired him $5,000 US for what the agency called a *general service fee*. In person he looked the way we'd expected, a bald man in his thirties, although surprisingly short. His head was perfectly hairless on top, but with brown tufts cut short around the ears and above his neck. He shook my hand very hard.

The parking lot overflowed with vehicles and people. As we seated ourselves in Nikolai's van, someone dropped a beer bottle from the taxi wedged beside us. The taxi lurched from its space, narrowly missing us, but Nikolai seemed unconcerned. His van was quite new, with a Kenmore stereo system. McDonald's wrappers from his kids' lunch littered the floor. I perched sideways in the front to see Nikolai as well as Betsy, and Betsy sat in the middle seat row, quiet, observant.

"What kind of music you like?" Nikolai asked me, grinning.

"Jazz and classical music," I said, not wanting to complicate things by mentioning Jimi Hendrix or Wilf Carter.

"Perfect," he said, like a waiter in a franchise restaurant back home. "I've got Chick Corea here." He turned it up loud. "You can buy this on CD for two dollars in the Kyiv market. Pretty good, yeah?"

I agreed and asked what other music he enjoyed. He said he listened to Michael Brecker and John Patituci but did not care for Louis Armstrong and "all those old guys." Nikolai started to tap out the drum part from the Corea album on his steering wheel.

"I play the drums," he said. He had a degree in music and was delighted to hear that I played the upright bass.

"You speak English very well," I said.

"I learn in California," he responded. He'd played drums in a big church there, but couldn't make a living as a musician in Ukraine. Now he no longer owned a drum kit. I thought of my dad, whose uncles insisted he do *something sensible* instead of being a musician. Nikolai was being sensible.

"Why you decide to adopt in Ukraine?" asked Nikolai.

"My father was born here. His family fled during World War II," I said.

"Did your father's family speak Ukrainian or Russian?"

"They spoke Russian and German, some spoke Ukrainian. My family was Mennonite. They pretended they were living somewhere else."

"What do you mean, somewhere else?"

"Well, at first Ukraine was like heaven for them, and then the revolution came and the wars. They thought they were in hell."

Nikolai laughed, showing all his white California teeth.

"Let me tell you a joke," he said. "An Englishman, a Frenchman and a Russian are at an art gallery looking at pictures of Adam and Eve in the garden. The Englishman says, 'Look, they're English — they're eating an apple for breakfast.' The Frenchman says, 'Look how beautiful they are naked — they must be French.' The Russian says, 'No, no — they have no clothes, almost nothing to eat, and they think they're in paradise — they must be Russians.'" Betsy's quietness was unusual, but throughout Nikolai had been addressing only me.

Then he spoke at a lower pitch, more seriously. "Guys, this is how it will work," he said. "It is hard to find healthy children to adopt right now. But I talk to my friends at the National Adoption Centre, they make phone calls, I help them, they help me."

Nikolai drove onto a sidewalk in a square crowded with people, trucks, motorcycles, stores, and bars. Someone waved him into a parking spot and he handed coins out the window. There were a few centimetres to spare on each side.

Nikolai helped take our luggage out of the van and walked us to the "Euro-style" flat that the agency had promised. As he opened the door to the stairwell at street level the briny smell of urine hit me. We picked our way up stairs cluttered with empty wine and vodka bottles. But the flat on the second floor, a collection of small apartments with a space for the manager in a central area, was clean and pleasant. Our unit had high ceilings, a balcony with wrought-iron railings, a bedroom, a kitchen, and a bathroom. It was also freezing cold.

The last thing we did that night was shop for breakfast foods in the mall across the street. The basement grocery store had every imaginable item, much of it from western Europe, and there was an enormous liquor section. We bought breakfast cereal and what we thought was milk; I'd left our *Lonely Planet* Ukrainian phrase book in the flat. But we'd bought *smetana*, and the following morning, shivering and tired, we found out *smetana* is sour cream.

▬▬

The next day, stuck inside Nikolai's Toyota van in slow-moving traffic, we gazed down at an old Lada. Nikolai said no one jokes about Ladas in Ukraine because that would be like making fun of a handicapped person. He enjoyed his own jokes.

Again he became solemn. "Guys," he said, "my friend at the National Adoption Centre has children for you. Two boys. They are great, great boys." He paused, waiting for us to react.

I turned from the front seat to look at Betsy. Our documents said we wanted to adopt one girl and a second child of either sex. Betsy had talked for years about how she wanted to raise a girl, and I could easily picture her passing on her feminist values to a daughter. At home I'd said either sex was fine so long as the children were healthy and toilet-trained.

"It's hard to find healthy children," Nikolai said, into our silence. "These two boys — they are great, and in the west."

When Betsy asked why the west was more desirable, he said that orphanages were smaller there than in other regions, and people drank less vodka. Most of the children were "social orphans" — abandoned by parents who couldn't afford to raise them.

What about fetal alcohol syndrome, we asked?

He grinned. "This is not Russia. We are a moral country, and not so many alcoholics."

—

That night, Betsy and I lay in bed in the darkness, our hands touching lightly. For a few minutes we didn't speak. We were here because in 2003, after three years of marriage, we'd decided to adopt children in Ukraine. I already had my nineteen-year-old son, Jeremy, whom we didn't see much, but Betsy and I really wanted to raise kids together.

In 2001 we'd bought a big old house in central Winnipeg that would hold our new family. I pictured being surrounded by my books, and our cats, and children who would look up to me and stay quiet while I wrote. My kids would have stable and predictable lives. And I would communicate my love to these children better than my father had to me. Or than I had to Jeremy. Betsy wanted to be a parent like her mother had been: enthusiastic, loving, and wise.

By 2002 we'd given up on the idea that she would get pregnant. We'd both had medical checks. Nothing was wrong. We saw a doctor at a fertility clinic. I was forty and Betsy only three years younger, which made bad odds for having a pregnancy through fertility treatments, and the treatments cost a lot.

I had just gutted my income by becoming a full-time writer. Betsy was an economics professor. Adoption made sense, and we knew a couple who had recently adopted children in Ukraine. They'd had much more control of the process than adoptive parents got in other countries, and we both had family roots in Ukraine. We began navigating paperwork and bureaucracy in 2003.

Then in 2004 Betsy got pregnant. The doctor said not to tell people until the end of the first trimester, and we didn't. We felt happy and scared, and talked to each other only a little about our hopes and fears for the baby, and mostly about the impact on the adoption. We decided to leave the adoption process open. All along we'd wanted more than one child.

The miscarriage came from nowhere: a sudden bleeding that didn't stop for days, and an undiscussable pain that gnawed for years afterward.

That year of the miscarriage I spent most days on the third floor of our house, writing, trying to write, avoiding writing. Betsy went to work, earned almost all the money, and left me with domestic chores that we'd agreed would compensate for my lost income. But I ruined her favourite dress pants by forgetting to read the care instructions, and frequently delayed emptying the dishwasher or putting the pots away, only to find her doing these chores when she got home. I felt guilty but also entitled to my new leisure after working for years at jobs that had seemed meaningless.

Betsy launched herself into various hobbies: pottery, stained glass, knitting, playing the piano. Sex, which had unfailingly brought us closer together in the past, began to seem military to me in Betsy's relentless focus on getting pregnant. She said her body, which she'd trained as a high school and college athlete, had never failed her before. The performance she most wanted now was not athletic though — it was reproduction.

We quarrelled. I accused her of ignoring me. She said it shouldn't be up to her to replace the attention that used to come from my colleagues at work. She pointed out that if I wasn't getting any writing done I should pay more attention to Jeremy's problems with school. We quarrelled about that too.

But there was still our shared project, the adoption. We had to work hard to persuade the Manitoba authorities to let us adopt in Ukraine. They were concerned about corruption, bribery, and worse. We had to explain to our friends that we weren't trying to save children from poverty. Our motives were more selfish. We wanted to adopt children for ourselves, for building our own family.

"Betsy," I said, tightening my grip on her hand as Kyiv's street noise filtered over us, "if we had biological children we'd have no control over their sex."

"That's true," she said. Through the wall a TV blared Ukrainian pop music.

"Could you be happy with boys?"

"Yes," she said, squeezing back, and I felt closer to her in that moment than I ever had to anyone. We went to sleep, drugged with jet lag.

At the National Adoption Centre on the morning of our interview, everything ran behind schedule. We waited two hours in a bare vestibule. Other prospective parents waited with us, Italians, Spaniards, Americans, all with their hired adoption facilitators. The waiting gave us time to think some more about the boys Nikolai had told us about, to wonder whether his friend had located a girl for us, and to realize yet again that we were not in control.

Finally Nikolai returned, beaming, from an extended series of visits down the long narrow hallway. We followed him into an office with two desks and a window at the end that had been patched with masking tape. Nikolai introduced us to his friend the psychologist, who wore an elegant powder-blue suit and looked like T.S. Eliot in old age. He quivered when he shook my hand.

The psychologist put three plastic-covered sheets on the desk. Two of them were held together with a paper clip that looked like an umbilical cord. These were the brothers Peter and Bohdan. They must be adopted together. We looked at their pictures. Peter, the five-year-old, had a mischievous grin, and he resembled one of my cousins. Three-year-old Bohdan's mouth turned down at the corners as if he had weights pulling on them.

The desk behind us was occupied now by the Americans. They studied an orange binder. "This child is very sick," their facilitator said. "She has had seizures probably caused by infection."

Nikolai translated the sketchy information about the boys on the plastic-lined sheets: their birth dates, when they were abandoned by their parents, the date when they arrived at the orphanage, their delayed development. We asked for their heights — *average for an orphanage.* The boys lived in Ternopil, near Poland. At first we heard "Chernobyl" for "Ternopil" and stared in blank confusion. Everyone smiled when Nikolai explained that Chernobyl was in a different part of the country.

The psychologist picked up the third plastic-covered sheet, on which we could see the picture of a little girl. As the psychologist read, he laughed, exposing his cigarette-stained teeth and stretching the liver spots on his cheeks. The girl's name was Halyna and she was six. She had dark hair and hazel eyes like my sister's. She lived to the south in Crimea. We had to choose between the boys and this little girl. The psychologist said something to Nikolai and then they both chortled. Nikolai explained this new joke. The parents' social status was recorded on every form by the orphanage director. In Halyna's case it just said *bums*, which is the same word in English, Russian, and Ukrainian. Her grandparents' social status was listed the same way: *bums*.

We felt stunned. As westerners who'd received an official letter that said we would have an interview, we expected one. Instead: adolescent jokes and fifteen minutes on hard wooden chairs in front of the psychologist's desk to make the most consequential decision of our lives.

"I want to meet the boys," said Betsy.

"Are you sure you'll be happy without a daughter?" I gazed steadily into her green eyes as if no one else was present. We were not approved to adopt three children.

"Orphanages are bigger in Crimea than in Ternopil," said Nikolai, exchanging a glance with the psychologist, "and they drink more vodka there — more Russians, you know."

Neither of us said anything.

"Guys, you need to make a decision. Other people . . ." and Nikolai nodded back to the lobby.

He had made the psychologist or someone more powerful hold these files for us. I guessed at the influence of the money we sent. Nikolai paced by the window in his black suit and the psychologist sat quietly, until after about ten minutes, we decided. Nikolai and the psychologist immediately began writing out documents in longhand. We were not legally committed to adopting the boys yet but they would be our sons unless some terrible problem turned up.

In an adjoining room, while Nikolai and the psychologist furiously scribbled, officials handed us more documents to sign, notarize, and copy. The first form read:

> Notice: To foreign prospective adoptive parents:
> This is to inform you that National Adoption Centre
> of Ministry of Education and Science of Ukraine will
> proceed with the process of adoption **without payment**.

I repressed my impulse to guffaw.

Betsy and I waited for Nikolai in the hallway. "Are you OK?" she said. I nodded and felt relieved that she'd noticed my distress. I did not want to choose. I closed my eyes and pictured a building with an infinite number of floors and a maze of hallways, exit signs, and rooms with children crying in their beds, alone, sweating with fever. The doors kept closing on officials signing documents, the conversations partly in German, the language of my early childhood. Once a door closed it never opened again.

Betsy and I decided to flip a coin because of my uncertainty, even though we'd already filled out the forms. "Call it," she said, and I called heads in the air for the boys. The Ukrainian coin landed on heads, trident-side up. Now our choice felt right.

Nikolai came back some indeterminate time later. When we asked about the little girl he said she'd already been selected by other people. No choice remained to second guess. I remembered a photograph of two of my cousins at the age the boys were now, in suits and crew-cuts, and how my mother always complained that they peed on the grate in aunt Lil's bathroom back in Winnipeg. I imagined teaching my younger son Bohdan to pee standing up.

▬

On the steaming hot train the next night, heading for Ternopil to meet our sons, I drank a beer in the dining car with Oleg, while Betsy read a novel in the sleeping compartment. Betsy read constantly, usually books I considered hopelessly middlebrow, but she enjoyed them. Oleg had just been hired by Nikolai as our adoption fixer and translator out in Ternopil. He lived in the eastern industrial city of Dnipropetrovsk, the same city where my dad's uncle Henry once attended university. A different world: 1941, the year Germany invaded the Soviet Union. Henry had to join the German army. His job was to translate the language of occupation for the *dirty, ignorant Slavs.*

Oleg had to translate for us, the ignorant Canadians. He was a fervid supporter of newly installed President Yushchenko and the Orange Revolution, which had just taken place and which proved to be his favourite topic of conversation, followed by how hard he worked and his love for God. Oleg was short and always in need of a shave. He spoke excellent English, quoted Shakespeare, and was a born-again Christian. He loved Whoppers, Pepsi, and George W. Bush. Previous clients, mostly wealthy Americans, had flown him to the new world where he saw professional sporting events and acquired a Dell laptop, a thumb drive, and a digital camera.

"Adopting in Ukraine," Oleg said to us, "is not like China. There it is Walmart. You pay, go to a hotel room, and they bring your baby girl to you all wrapped up with a bow on her head. Here you have to do a lot of work." He seemed to relish the idea of us doing a lot of work. Betsy and I grinned at each other when he couldn't see.

Then he told us that Peter and Bohdan, the brothers we expected to adopt, lived in different orphanages, 140 kilometres apart. According to what the National Adoption Centre had told us, both boys were in Ternopil. But that information was a year out of date.

Oleg went to his compartment to make calls on his cell phone. I went to sleep in our compartment reading *Barbarossa*, Alan Clark's book on the German invasion of the Soviet Union. All the atrocity stories were in footnotes.

II

Oleg, Betsy and I arrived at the Ternopil train station just before daybreak. During the trip from Kyiv, Oleg had found a flat for us. Our new landlord met us at the station wearing an Adidas tracksuit stretched tightly around his barrel-shaped body. He drove us in a shiny silver van down unlit streets to the edge of a lake, and stopped at his apartment building. The entrance housed feral cats whose acrid smell lingered after them and dissipated as we climbed the stairs, though the odour stayed imprinted on my mind the way that certain family stories did.

The flat felt luxurious, with hardwood floors and textured concrete walls in swirling wave patterns. The bathroom was tiled in purple and yellow, the kitchen was well-equipped to prepare meals, there was cable TV, and we had two bedrooms so Oleg didn't have to sleep on the couch. Best of all, the flat had a working furnace, unlike our place in Kyiv. We slept for two hours before Oleg knocked on our door at 7:30 am.

From the kitchen window I could see the first winter sun glinting on the frozen lake below, which was decorated with iron-filigreed railings, Greek pillars, and a bridge. Part of the lake was a crater carved out by German bombing in World War II, the war that had driven my father and his family, possibly through this very place, to Poland. My new family would begin in this scarred and wintry city.

We expected to meet our sons immediately that morning. Instead Oleg took us on a paper chase for almost our entire first day in Ternopil. In our rush to get out of Kyiv, Nikolai had forgotten to prepare the power of attorney that Oleg needed to act on our behalf in the adoption. Therefore we now had to notarize a back-dated version of the power of attorney. This was illegal but not the real problem. Oleg spotted a notary's office, and we walked in to see a lineup of old women, businessmen, boys with tight tapered jeans and cell phones, all of them waiting.

After twenty minutes it was our turn. The notary sat like a high priest in silence behind a giant mahogany desk and a computer. She gestured to us to sit, and Oleg stood in front of her, almost as if he were auditioning, and spoke for a long time. The notary responded in a couple of clipped sentences, with great emphasis on the last one. Oleg explained the problem to us: he did not have the document he needed in this region showing that he was a government-approved interpreter. Also, the notary didn't like the idea of Oleg acting on our behalf for the adoption, even though Oleg assured us later that this was normal.

We walked back into the slushy, narrow streets. Around the town square we saw a theatre that staged Ukrainian plays, a cathedral, and brightly-painted apartments that had iron railings on the balconies. I smelt beer, cigarettes, fried foods, diesel exhaust, laundry drying in the crisp air, and my stomach rumbled for lunch. Oleg walked at speed on his short legs from one office to another, all over Ternopil's complicated streets. Possibly he enjoyed making us chase him. Betsy was more resilient than I, and with her long legs she could walk faster than Oleg, but she exchanged nervous glances with me.

In the end we saw the inner sanctums of another four notaries, who all turned us down with the same degree of haughtiness. We also spent half an hour at city hall while Oleg talked to officials and we said *dyakuyu*, thank you, to anyone who looked important.

"I love this town," Oleg said. "I love the fahny way they talk out here. It's fahn just to watch the people. But I don't like the notaries. Oh, the notaries." He shook his head like Job contemplating God's perversity.

By late afternoon Oleg had abandoned the quest for a notary. Sometime during our whirlwind office tour he'd acquired the local referral we needed to see Bohdan. We were finally driving in a taxi to the Ternopil Specialized Children's Home at the edge of town. The winter sun set as we entered the orphanage director's office. He was a big, heavyset man with a dour manner and a black fur cap glued to his head. He pointed to a poster on the wall of newly elected President Yushchenko at Independence Square, waving to an ecstatic crowd. Oleg chatted rapidly with him, and we assumed it was about politics.

The director shook our hands with a terrifying grip, smiled for the first time, and began telling us about Bohdan through Oleg's translation. At birth Bohdan had measured eight points on the APGAR scale, a flourishing baby. But the parents abused alcohol and lived in "a bad psychological atmosphere." Bohdan's mother abandoned him and Peter two years ago, and lost her parental rights after twice failing to appear in court. Their father had disappeared long before. Bohdan entered the orphanage at one year and three months old. He had various "disorders of development," meaning that he had talked and walked late. He'd had bronchitis and an ear infection in the last year. "He likes to be tenderly treated," said the director, reading from a doctor's report, and he smiled more warmly than before.

After the meeting we walked down a series of long under-heated hallways, all very clean and adorned with the occasional plant or a portrait of Ukraine's national poet, Taras Shevchenko. The director led us up a flight of stairs and into a bare white entranceway. Through the doorway we watched as a group of children gathered around him. A worker in a white smock and kerchief with prominent gold teeth came leading one boy from the group. It was Bohdan. "This is your mama and papa," she said in Ukrainian.

Bohdan's brown eyes glowed like deep pools of chocolate. His mouth turned down at the edges as if he was thinking hard or about to cry. He wore a royal blue Indianapolis Colts sweatsuit. Betsy and I looked at each other, delighted. We were both born in Indiana when our fathers were in graduate school, only thirty miles apart, though we didn't meet for another thirty-three years. What a bizarre coincidence, to meet our son wearing this emblem of our accidentally shared home state, a world away from the midwestern us. It had to be a good omen.

Anya, the worker who'd led Bohdan out to see us, said "Mama," and whispered something to him. When we sat down she plopped him on Betsy's lap. Betsy handed him a lollipop that he stuck quickly in his mouth. Bohdan grinned at her and then at me. Betsy and I started to tear up. Could this beautiful child be our son? The other kids clamoured, all eager to be held and touched. We gave them lollipops too.

Anya removed Bohdan's candy and he began reciting what Oleg said was a prayer. Every minute or so he got stuck and Anya prompted him to continue the lengthy recitation. She gestured to us as he continued, as if to say see, he is a bright boy. Some of his mates did not look so capable. A number of them had the facial markers of fetal alcohol syndrome, which we'd memorized back home. Oleg took pictures with his digital camera and chatted with the workers and children.

Bohdan relaxed in my lap for a long time. I stroked his head and tickled him. His whole being lit up with pleasure. He crinkled his eyes and chuckled. Oleg told me that the name *Bohdan* means "God's gift" in the Slavic languages.

On Saturday morning we met Bohdan for the second time. He picked out our voices in the entryway, and we heard him shouting. Anya ran out, smiling, and spoke rapidly to Oleg, who translated: "I asked him why he was running, and he said 'My daddy has come for me.'" I wondered whether he said this because, like all children, he wanted a father, or if it was because he loved me already. Then one of the mentally challenged kids jumped through the doorway, sporting the same Indianapolis Colts outfit Bohdan had worn the previous day. The kids wore whatever clothes came to hand.

Except for a couple of hour-long visits with Bohdan, Betsy and I were alone in our flat for most of the weekend. Betsy did the meal planning and cooking, while I did the dishes. Oleg spent the whole weekend driving the 140 kilometres back and forth to a town near Peter's orphanage, making arrangements with district officials for documents we needed before we could meet Peter. Bohdan seemed like a perfect son for us, and in excellent health, but if Peter wasn't healthy enough for Canadian immigration, we would not be able to adopt either of them. Then Oleg told us that Peter was in the orphanage infirmary because of an accident.

On Monday morning we left to meet Peter in the small white cab of our regular taxi driver, Andrey. Betsy and I wedged into the back seat, in spite of us both being a foot taller than Oleg. Outside Ternopil, in the early morning chill, the landscape was flat and curtains of fog obscured the horizon. The countryside reminded me of the prairies in North America, with snow-covered fields, windbreaks, desolate highways. But every few kilometres there was a village filled with what to us were exotic sights: cathedrals crowned by shining cupolas, crumbling brick buildings, textured concrete fences painted two-tone, in Easter egg colours. The roads wound in narrow cobblestone, rattling our bones and teeth. Stray dogs and ragged people jaywalked, carrying Hugo Boss shopping bags. As we drove out of each settlement a sign appeared with the place name stroked out, as if God reached down and expunged everything except the fields and the miniature roadside cathedrals where you could pray for protection.

After two hours' driving we stopped in the last major town before Peter's orphanage and ate cold pizza for breakfast. Then we waited in the car while Oleg tried to find an official. We needed a local referral to see Peter, even though we already had one from Kyiv. Before leaving the apartment I'd given Oleg $300 Ukrainian, for "expediting expenses." We didn't know how much of our money was going into expediting, only that we had cashed out our savings and extended our line of credit for the adoptions. Now we waited in the frigid cab while Oleg expedited and talked politics. After a while he called us in to meet the official who would issue the referral.

The public buildings were all the same: rambling hallways with high ceilings, peeling paint, crucifixes and political posters on the walls above eye level, no detectable heat from the radiators, and dirty bathrooms without toilet seats or paper. Workers kept their fur hats on all day. When I left a building last I usually violated Ukrainian etiquette by failing to close the door behind me. Oleg looked at me darkly, implying that I was a lazy Canadian, someone who expected doors to close themselves.

We took a back road out of town, and soon the pavement became gravel. As the road descended into the Dniester river valley, the fog cleared away and the Carpathian mountains appeared across the river. Soon we saw the village where Peter lived. It was called Koropets, *carp*. A sculpture of the rotund, scaly fish protruded obscenely from beside the road. We stopped and took pictures of each other beside the fish. Oleg said, "God is good," because of the sunshine washing the foothills of western Ukraine, and I felt a surge of gratitude and hope. Soon we drove past a creek onto the orphanage grounds. On our left was an old, ornate building that Andrey said had been a Polish count's palace long ago.

———

As we stepped out of the taxi, Oleg motioned at us officiously while chatting on his cell phone to someone. We entered a low building on our right and Oleg introduced us to the orphanage director, a short, middle-aged woman wearing a skirt and fashionable boots. She smiled warmly and led us to the infirmary, a small room with three beds.

Peter lay on the bed nearest the door, in a light blue turtleneck and sweatpants. He had a block-shaped head, long eyelashes, and luminescent silver-green eyes under short brown hair. His face was pudgy and handsome; right between his eyebrows was a big x-shaped bandage. He had just awakened.

Another child pushed Peter into the bedpost last night, the director explained, just at the time Oleg phoned to say we were coming. It was an accident. But Peter had needed three stitches to close the wound.

The orphanage director seated herself on Peter's bed and stroked his hair. She said *mom and dad* a few times, the only words that I understood. Peter looked at us with his eyes pulsing. Then Oleg spoke to him, and Peter responded with a high-pitched, rapid-fire barrage of words that Oleg translated.

"I dreamed about an elephant, a bear, and a fox, in a big forest," Peter said. "I was running and scared. And then I slept in my bed. Down the road through the forest came my mother and father, to take me away." He smiled and I noticed that his ears stuck out. Betsy looked at me with tears tracking down her cheeks. I decided to kill anyone who might laugh at Peter's bandage even if his broad forehead did remind me of Frankenstein.

Through Oleg, Betsy asked Peter if he had any brothers or sisters.

"Yes, I have a baby brother, Bohdan! Where is he? Can I see him?"

Oleg said that he'd have to wait, and showed Peter a picture of Bohdan on his digital camera. Peter's face lit up with joy.

"Pampushka!" he said, laughing and pointing at Bohdan's fleshy cheeks in the picture. *Pampushka*, Oleg explained, were little garlic buns. Bohdan had put on baby fat in the orphanage.

As I stood there staring at Peter, I thought of my father's escape from eastern Germany in 1945: a little boy, running to a soundtrack of Russian rifle fire through a beet field, running toward safety and the death of his mother.

Peter held a plastic bag that contained all his property — a scribbler filled with doodles, a single wooden block, and the candy we'd given him. He sat in Betsy's lap, chattering as if she understood him. Then he plunked himself on my lap. He clutched my hand to his chest like he was afraid of drowning in the open air, pulled my arms tight around him, talking and talking without a pause for breath. Oleg was no longer translating but I didn't care. The words no longer signified in their *meaning*. It seemed to me then that Peter experienced the world as I did, as words that tumbled out of mouths or fingers, not always under control, giant numbers of them like space probes sent to meet the other sentient beings that must be out there somewhere. We'd made contact.

III

Having met our sons, we now expected to finish the legal process within a week, after Oleg collected the required documents and the regional court approved our adoptions.

But our expectations for a speedy conclusion were shattered. For the next three weeks, Betsy and I waited and waited while Oleg piled up documents for the adoption dossiers and had them notarized. Another wrinkle: Peter's orphanage doctor had told us about Peter getting a positive skin test for tuberculosis. While the doctor said this was no cause for concern, we knew that Peter must pass a medical exam for Canadian immigration.

Early in the month Oleg took us in Andrey's cab to bow and scrape in front of local officials. We visited the boys whenever we could, which was especially hard with Peter, his orphanage hours away on a bad winter road. The time crawled. Even once the court approved our adoptions, we'd still have a thirty-day waiting period before we could take custody of our sons, according to Ukrainian law.

We spent part of each day killing time in an Internet café near the flat, sending emails to our family and friends at home, and eagerly looking for answers. Everyone except Jeremy responded immediately with congratulations on our new family. My dad sent us this message:

Hi Maurice & Betsy!

Thanks for keeping us so well informed about your Ukraine journey. We now have a clear, sharp picture and understand what it is you've been doing and what still remains to be done. And we are becoming anxious with you for the ultimate conclusion to happen a.s.a.p. We are all very excited about meeting Peter & Bohdan with their new parents.

. . .

Every day we await further updating.

Our love to you ALL, mom & dad.

Coming from my father, this was expansive and emotional. I felt grateful. Then, after some cajoling and a phone call by my sister, Jeremy responded to my second message:

News sounds great! First of all, I don't think you should anglicize Petro, it's a far cooler name than Peter. Second of all, who wouldn't want a big brother like me? Third, Bohdan's a damn good name too.

. . .

The kids sound spunky.

Love, Jeremy

I felt relief and sweat run down my body as I read his message. Back home Jeremy had said he wanted to have brothers, but his non-response to my messages had filled me with anxiety. His impulse to argue about everything, even Peter's name, was exactly like mine. We hadn't always been like that.

I remembered sitting with Jeremy when he was four in our living room, facing a small park across the street. I held him up and we picked our topics from whatever came in sight.

"Look, it's a car! The car drives. *The car drives.*"

"Caw. Caw. Caw dwive."

"*The car drivezz.*"

"The caw dwivezz."

"Good! Very good! How about this. *The bird flies.*"

"The buhd fliezz." I hugged him to my chest and put my hands on his cheeks, feeling like Rex Harrison in *My Fair Lady.* I could feel the perfectly smooth skin of his arms and breathe in the fresh bread smell of his body. His straw-coloured stringy blonde hair came from his mother. We both laughed like idiots. I loved my son.

On the morning of February 11, our cell phone's alarm went off at 6:00 am. The plan was to leave for Peter's orphanage at 6:30, and to take him for more blood tests — we weren't sure exactly what for. I'd promised Betsy to get up and dance if she set the phone to play "Latin Loop." My genetic heritage molded me for sitting in a pew, not for fluid hip movements to a Latin beat. Betsy cracked up. It had been weeks since we'd had an argument about anything.

When we picked Peter up at the orphanage we saw his dormitory for the first time. The stitches were out of his wound, so he had been released from the infirmary. Now he wore a smaller bandage on his forehead. He got very angry at me when I didn't let him play with our cell phone.

An orphanage worker named Oksana came along with us, displacing Oleg from the front of the cab and holding Peter on her lap. She asked us for a plastic bag as soon as we got in the taxi, and draped a towel over her shoulder. This was standard procedure: orphanage children had little experience with driving, and they tended to vomit. For the first few minutes Peter chattered continuously. Oleg translated some of it — Peter was excited about seeing how cars and trucks used their turn signals and brake lights. Within a few more minutes, Peter was quiet and pale. Oksana took off his jacket to cool him. Soon she asked Andrey to drive slowly on the hills. Then the taxi stopped. Oksana took Peter out and he threw up at the edge of the road. She wiped his face with the towel and they got back in. We continued to drive slowly. At the next town I bought some kind of pill at a pharmacy where they sold medication one tablet at a time. It wasn't the Gravol we asked for, since Peter had to stop and puke several more times.

▬

Because of our slow pace and frequent stops, getting to Ternopil took an extra hour over the usual two. On the outskirts of town we stopped at a big brick building. A sign in both Ukrainian and English said Tuberculosis Hospital. Oleg had only told us about blood tests, so we were surprised by this stop. We didn't know what treatment Peter had been given for his positive skin test for TB.

Inside the hospital the lights were turned off, presumably to save money. In the artificial twilight of the hallways we saw cadaverous men and women in light cotton gowns, making deep chest coughs. Peter greeted a passing nurse by name, and stopped to ask Oleg about a cart that carried food trays. He talked to a patient. He had been here before.

Oksana led us to a corner office decorated with patterned concrete. Peter was briefly taken away for a chest x-ray by a young woman with embroidered jeans under a white lab coat and a tall chef's hat. She was Tatiana, the junior doctor. Maria was the doctor in charge, an older woman, short and round, in an even taller chef's hat. When Peter came back with Tatiana, he gave Maria a hug. It turned out Peter had been an outpatient here for three months, getting the drug isoniazid as a preventive treatment for TB. He'd never had any symptoms of active disease. Oleg told Dr. Maria about the adoption. She held Peter and cried. Tatiana had to adjust her makeup because she was crying too.

Oleg wanted to get going, but Betsy and I insisted on exchanging addresses with the doctors. They both stood with Peter for a picture, and we promised to send it to them. All of us wept except Peter and Oleg. We left when the x-ray of Peter's lungs came back. It was very small, the size x-rays were in the 1940s, when my father was checked for TB after the war. Lil had told me about them.

Oleg said we must leave immediately for Peter's blood tests. We went to a clinic a few blocks into Ternopil. Oksana, who was rather proprietary about holding Peter, let Betsy hold him for the blood withdrawal. His face scrunched up gradually, like a digital picture breaking up, and he cried quietly. But he smiled as soon as it was over. We gave him a Hot Wheels car that we'd bought in Ternopil and he was thrilled.

Next Andrey drove us across town to drop off a form at Bohdan's orphanage. Peter asked Oleg, very quietly, if he could see Bohdan, but Oksana wouldn't allow that. She also explained that Betsy and I could not see Bohdan because it was nap time and the orphanage workers didn't like the routines interrupted. Andrey dropped Betsy and me off at our flat, and drove back to Koropets with Peter, Oksana, and Oleg.

▬

The next day we visited Bohdan again. He held a spoonful of yogurt out to me and when I reached for it with my mouth he withdrew the spoon suddenly and grinned. He rarely laughed out loud.

Oleg had to take a picture of Bohdan for Canadian immigration.

"*Odin, dva, tri,*" he said, counting. Then the digital camera made a little whistling sound, and Bohdan frowned, unfamiliar with the expectations. Betsy began laughing.

"*Odin, dva, tri,*" went Oleg, again, after instructing Bohdan on how to smile. No go. On his fifth try, Oleg got Bohdan to protrude his lower teeth. By then I was laughing too, and so was the orphanage worker. This would be his official immigration photo.

▬

Most days Betsy cooked frozen mushroom and fruit perogies on a gas burner, cut up tough rye bread and spooned out the delicious local yogurt, moving quickly around in the tiny kitchen, her work fluid and efficient, her body slender and strong. She had also established an exercise routine early in the mornings that involved running outside and calisthenics inside. With her athletic background, she had an insatiable passion for working out that I never understood. She was three years younger than I and maybe that difference accounted for her energy level.

Often in the evening I felt so exhausted I just watched Ukrainian and Russian music videos on TV. One showed a chorus of young women singing in black dresses with deep v-slits exposing their breasts. They played air cellos while they sang. The lead singer sat naked on a white couch with a large egg in her lap, while a man danced around the woman, plucking air strings with his bare feet. The music sounded like Boney M. Betsy came into the room and shook her head, torn between disapproval and amusement.

On Valentine's Day Betsy and I exchanged cards that we'd bought in Winnipeg. In the afternoon we had what she called a *tryst*; at home I referred to sex as "fooling around," but tryst was much better. Our relationship felt romantic again, like a shared adventure.

On February 15 the day started well — we saw Bohdan and about a dozen other kids in the Ternopil orphanage perform a spring concert. There was a gap-toothed girl who wore white ribbons bigger than her head and a white dress with a matching cape. Beside her was a boy dressed in yellow with a cardboard crown cut like a huge sun. He protruded his stomach from his hips like a skinny Pickwick and made long recitations. His queen had braids in her blonde hair and no lines to say. The kids sang songs, shouting them out with a piano. The room where the performance took place was a chapel, and an orthodox priest attended in full regalia behind an altar. Bohdan glanced at us, looking quite detached from the proceedings. The kids fixated on a basket brought in by the queen — it was full of candies for them. One of the workers said Bohdan wanted to go to Canada right away.

The moment the spring concert ended we called Oleg and drove to Koropets, where we picked up Peter, the orphanage director, and the orphanage lawyer. We were due in a nearby town for the guardianship committee hearing. Normally these committees rubber-stamped foreign adoptions if the paperwork looked good and the correct disbursements had gone out.

There was no chance for lunch. We arrived after two o'clock and then sat in a small office crowded with furniture, icons, and pictures of a social worker's family. We watched as various staff came and went and made calls on a rotary phone for about an hour. They were investigating Peter and Bohdan's half-brother, Viktor, who was twenty-one. They had managed to locate him in a remote village about an hour away, unemployed and living with an aunt. Peter sat beside me playing with pens and paper. While I watched people scurry in and out and exchanged helpless shrugs with Betsy, Peter grabbed a battery-operated clock from the social worker's desk. He removed a set-screw from the back and was about to take apart the whole clock when I noticed him and took it away. He held the set-screw and gestured at the clock. I put it back in his lap to see what he'd do. Peter re-threaded the screw back into the tiny hole with surprising speed.

The hearing began sometime in the late afternoon. It was held in a large room. We sat in hard chairs near the door with Oleg to translate, and to our right sat twelve women, the guardianship committee, along the wall. Directly facing the door, on a diagonal, were two desks pushed together in an L. At the bigger one was the chair of the meeting. The women began asking questions, directing them at me, the only man in the room other than Oleg. They asked about our household income, about my payments to my ex-wife, about our mortgage, all information they already should have had. It appeared they didn't believe we could support the boys financially. They also wanted to know what my son Jeremy thought of having siblings. I said he liked the idea. One of the women, who spoke a little English, wanted to know why we did not have children "of our own." Betsy started to answer, and the chairperson cut her short. They didn't need to know this, she said.

They asked why we were adopting in Ukraine and I gave them a speech about family roots, and coming from Winnipeg, the capital of the Ukrainian diaspora, where we could preserve the boys' heritage, all of it perfectly sincere. Then the second official, the one Oleg called "the mean lady," asked how we would care for the boys while we worked. I said we'd take turns — one of us would always be with the kids — a lie that no one challenged. I felt like asking for a show of hands on how many of these women did all their own childcare.

Instead I said, "We consider the boys a sacred trust and we appreciate that you take the adoption as seriously as we do." A woman in a grey smock asked what kind of books I wrote. I tried to describe them: poetry that um, explored language and the past, also a non-fiction book about TB. None of them rolled their eyes. Then Betsy, Oleg, and I were dismissed to the small office while the committee deliberated.

When we returned they told us that they approved of us as parents. However, they could not approve the adoption until the boys' brother Viktor gave his consent. Then Oleg launched into a big argument with them about Ukrainian adoption law. A number of the women had copies of a legal book, about the size of a Gideons New Testament, that they waved aggressively in front of Oleg's face. He was wearing his suit and had severe five o'clock shadow. His red tie made his face look angry. I realized he was losing the argument. He went out and made a phone call.

We pushed ourselves into Andrey's taxi then and set off to find Viktor. Mila, a local official who had been very helpful, went with us. Peter cried when we dropped him off at the orphanage. Betsy and I felt awful watching him, even though Oleg assured us he knew that we would come back. How did Peter know that?

His own mother abandoned him, his dad was God knows where, and we were strangers who did not speak his language from a country he could not even imagine.

We had no time for dinner. There was snow and haze on the narrow, darkening roads, and I could feel my stomach shrinking into knots of anxiety and hunger. What if Viktor didn't give his consent? I checked my wallet, worried that Viktor would want money.

We stopped three different times to ask for directions at the roadside. At 7:30, in complete darkness, we entered Viktor's village. Oleg told Betsy and me not to speak, and to stay in the cab, hunched down. He was afraid someone might try to extort money from us for Viktor's signature. With the motor off, the cab felt like an arctic tomb.

I imagined going back to Kyiv and starting over, seeing tiny pictures of other children about whom we would know almost nothing. How empty that would feel compared to what I knew from holding Peter and Bohdan on my lap.

At the ninety-minute mark Betsy called Oleg on his cell. He sent a text message saying he was almost done. Back in the car, the "signature" Oleg had gotten was actually five handwritten copies of a statement saying that Viktor had never met his brothers and had no objection to the adoption. Oleg also had gotten the head of the village council to sign each copy. Apparently we needed this elaborate documentation because Viktor had no birth certificate or passport.

We drove back and ate at our regular restaurant outside Ternopil. It was well after eleven. The mushroom perogies and dark beer had never tasted so good.

The next day I felt hungover and groggy. It had been almost two weeks since we'd arrived in Ternopil and we had expected to be going home by now. We saw Bohdan at most one hour each day and Peter only once or twice a week because of the long drive out to the country. Our flat cost $60 US a night with an additional charge for the laundry. I was losing weight. Betsy had the cold that I'd already recovered from.

IV

In the last week of February we said goodbye to the boys. We had to go home for the mandated thirty-day waiting period after our court cases because we'd already exceeded our budget, and Betsy was needed at work. Her parental leave could only begin when we took legal custody of the boys. These complicated arrangements were hard enough to explain to our friends and relatives, never mind to Peter and Bohdan.

Oleg had not phoned ahead to Peter's orphanage as he should have, so when we arrived, Peter was napping and had to be wakened. We gave him a second Hot Wheels car, this one with a wolverine character painted on the roof. He played with a key chain of mine and, under her close supervision, with Betsy's Swiss Army knife. He drank from a juice box after a lot of fiddling with the straw. We left him a letter and pictures of himself with us, and us with his brother Bohdan. Until we had legal custody of them both, he would not be allowed to see his brother in person.

Oleg was obviously bored with his job at this point. His early enthusiasm and enjoyment of the children were gone. We pled with him to help us talk to Peter. Oleg explained to him that we'd be back when the snow melted, which Peter seemed to understand, although I wondered if he really believed us.

Peter showed us his bed, in a row where the other kids were still waking up, groggy in the late afternoon from their long nap.

Peter ran around noisily showing off the pictures and his new toy car. When the kids got up they immediately headed to us. A little girl who howled instead of speaking sat on Betsy's lap; in a moment she pulled Betsy's hair as hard as she could. I lost count of all the children who sat on my lap. Some were quiet, happy for the physical contact and attention from an adult. Others flailed their limbs around and pinched my arms.

Oleg helped us talk to one of Peter's teachers, a middle-aged woman named Zaryana in a wool sweater and skirt.

"You must love him like your soul but shake him like a pear tree," she said. Oleg told us this was a folk saying that referred to children who are good but need some firmness to keep them in line. Zaryana said Peter had learned only half the alphabet because he fooled around so much in class. Betsy and I thought he just needed more individual attention, as did the doctors who'd seen him. There were too many kids in his orphanage group for the number of workers, and some of them had severe disabilities.

We exchanged addresses with Zaryana and promised to keep in touch. She referred to us as "normal" parents, and when we asked why, she said it was because we wanted to adopt both brothers. We didn't mention that it was legally impossible to adopt only one of them. Normal was great.

Normal was what I had worked so hard for with Jeremy in his early teens, driving him to music lessons, punctuating the long rides with lectures on the joy of hard work, arguing with him about why he didn't visit more often after his mother refused to negotiate custody arrangements. I pictured Jeremy sitting now at his computer, pale, listening to MP3 tracks on his headset, oblivious to the world outside.

There were two workers named Anya at Bohdan's orphanage, and the morning shift was covered by Anya with the gold teeth. She brought Bohdan out to us in the hallway so we could say good-bye to him. As in many public buildings they avoided turning any lights on during the day. I picked Bohdan up so he could reach the light switch. He flipped it to on, and a bare light bulb glared down at us.

"On," I said.

"Uhn," he said.

"Off," I said, flipping it off.

"Uhff," he said, and chortled. Anya was staring at us disapprovingly. She spoke rapidly to Bohdan in Ukrainian, then pointed downward at the switch. I nodded agreeably. We would not play with the light switches.

Anya brought us some toys from a closet in the hall. There was a stuffed dog, a book, a truck, and a few other stuffed animals. Bohdan picked those up, and also collected Betsy's watch. He carried them to the far corner of the room, where the kids had their lockers. Using words and hand gestures he told me and Betsy to stay away.

Bohdan sat down with the book and managed to tear half a page out of it. Betsy's face registered amusement at my horror. The book was a children's reader from 1980, Soviet times, with a picture of Lenin hugging a child.

We left Bohdan with a letter and photographs. Anya told Oleg that they would read the letter to Bohdan and go over the pictures with him in the month we'd be gone. We hugged and kissed him. Before we left he picked up Oleg's briefcase, which contained something like 300 pages of legal documents, a book about our sons. He was a strong boy. But he was only three and he didn't understand *until the snow melts*.

On one of the days leading up to our court hearings I went, for the first time, on a morning run with Betsy. Her route went down the river walk and over the icy bridge. I didn't have sweatpants or headgear for running, so I tied a tea towel with a bright yellow pattern around my bald head and wore Betsy's pajama pants. Her legs are longer than mine, even though I'm over six feet tall, and I had to hitch the pants up on my waist. No one stared at me; instead, they seemed to look through me, and through Betsy too; there were no other runners. Afterward we went to the Internet café and the grocery store.

Then came bad news from Nikolai in Kyiv: the woman who directed the National Adoption Centre had withheld her signature from all documents on the exact day we needed them for the court hearings. She was angry because her husband had just been fired by the new Yushchenko government. Apparently he was high up in what Ukrainians still called the KGB — the internal security service, a recognized nexus of corrupt officials and organized crime. Nikolai thought this would blow over within three days, but it meant we had to re-book our return flight to Canada for later in the week. There was no guarantee that the director would do anything on a predictable schedule, but Nikolai said, "Her pride will make her do it — she has a policy of signing all documents within four working days."

———

That night I was filling in documents, with some help from Betsy, on Oleg's laptop, because Oleg didn't feel like doing them. Actually, since we put his name on them, we were forging Canadian immigration documents, and making up cheerful answers to questions we weren't sure of. I worked at the kitchen table and Betsy sat opposite me reading some unreadable novel. She'd already had her shower and was in her wind-down mode.

"What do I put for Peter's birthplace?" I'd fallen into the habit of letting Betsy keep track of such details while I dreamed of writing a book about my adopted sons.

"You're going to have to look it up," she said.

"Why did you ask me to do this if you aren't willing to help?"

"You volunteered because you said I was doing too much. So now you have to do some work."

A couple of minutes passed while I shuffled papers to get her attention.

"I found the documents with Peter's birthplace. But we'll have to get Oleg to translate this one."

"I told you before that one's already translated. Are you listening to me at all?" Betsy snapped.

"Don't get all touchy. I need your help — take a look at this."

"You want to look incompetent so you can go back to taking notes for your book."

Then she called me Eric. I called her a bitch. She told me to fuck off. I stomped out of the room, abandoning the Eurasian continent for the tropical shower. When I came to bed she was already asleep.

We were both sick of the delay, which might be putting our adoption in jeopardy, and was definitely costing us hundreds of dollars. We were sick of Oleg too. The only good news was that he'd be going back home to Dnipropetrovsk while we waited for the director to sign our final document. The bad news was that once he left, it would be just the two of us.

V

It was February 25, the day I would become Peter and Bohdan's father, and Betsy their mother. We woke up at 6:30 am in our Ternopil flat. We'd have two court hearings to legalize the adoption of our sons. Then we'd drive back to the flat, pack our things, and drive all night to fly home from Kyiv.

In Ternopil for Bohdan's hearing we were ushered into a courtroom with whitewashed walls, hard wooden benches, and the blue and yellow Ukrainian trident hanging on the front wall. Other than the trident, the stark room resembled a Mennonite church from before the war. The judge was a young man in a turtleneck, with a high-pitched voice. The chief prosecutor was a woman and she sat in front of the judge. We sat beside Oleg, our bench facing the judge, the prosecutor, and a recording secretary.

Immediately behind us sat the doctor from Bohdan's orphanage and the woman in charge of orphanages in the region. Both kept their large fur coats on. The doctor got up when the judge prompted her. Oleg translated her testimony in a whisper: Bohdan "had an improved psychological state" when he knew we would adopt him.

"This means he is happier," said Oleg.

Because Ukrainian law recognized the man as household head, I was prepared to do most of the talking. In the cab Betsy had told me I should make sure to look the judge in the eye when speaking since my shyness in public can make me look evasive, even dishonest. But the judge asked the same questions as all the other hearings, to which I gave the same answers while trying to look trustworthy and conscientious. After a twenty-minute recess he came back with a document approving our adoption of

Bohdan. I had a new son and joyful music sounded in my mind —
Charlie Parker playing "Yardbird Suite."

Now we had to drive three hours to Koropets for Peter's
court case. Betsy and I held hands for a while and then settled
back into our cramped seat space in the taxi without talking.
Snow fell on the winding country roads, swirling in the wind
and blanking out the view. Sometimes a truck emerged from the
snow and I heard a displaced roar as it went past.

During the long drive to Koropets on the snow-covered highway
the cab tires hummed softly and smoothly at concert A pitch, the
same sound I remembered from childhood, driving on the Dis-
raeli Freeway to my aunt Lil's house back in Winnipeg, before
they paved the bridges smooth and quiet. I associated that hum-
ming sound with stories about the war, the same stories over and
over but full of gaps and Dickensian coincidences.

As an adult, when I started a book about my family history,
I drove twice on the now-silent bridges over the Red River to
North Kildonan to see how many gaps my aunt could fill. She
told me the whole story, her hand shaking on the coffee pot, her
black hair turned perfectly white.

By 1944, Lil and my father were living on a beautiful estate
fifty kilometres from Berlin with their mother Helen and her in-
laws. Helen had married a German agricultural officer, Helmut
Simon, whom she'd met in Ukraine. They'd spent most of 1943
travelling west with the retreating German army.

The two-storey Simon house overlooked a small lake and
tall chestnut trees. The house had three balconies, and summer
guests went rowing on the lake. The Simons made some extra
money putting up these tourists. Helen's in-laws lived on the
main floor, along with the city folks. In the basement Mrs. Simon,

Helmut's mother, cooked for everyone. Helen, Dad, and Lil lived on the second floor. Lil and my father enjoyed living in the house, on the big estate. They even attended school for a few months. In early June cherries and strawberries ripened along the lakeshore.

Then Germany began to conscript all available men to replace the millions of dead soldiers in the east. In 1944, Simon was called up. Helen had just given birth to the only child she had with Simon — baby Helmut was six weeks old when his father left in the fall.

Simon wrote home from the front in Stettin in 1945, on a *Feldpostkarte* or "postcard from the field." The postcard said: "I am an ordinary soldier, which I thought I'd never be in my life again."

There was nothing ordinary about the eastern front. The Germans had killed ninety-seven percent of Russian POWs, and the Red Army rank and file knew that. There were no more postcards from Simon. Rumours flew about the Soviet advance on Berlin and about the barbarism of the soldiers. The Simon estate was directly in the Soviet army's path to Berlin.

What my father remembers about the day the Red Army invaded appears in flashes, fragments that he has shown me over the years. He was playing beside the lake with a toy truck, just like any other day, when a Russian plane came out of the sky, giant, noisy, strafing the trees with bullets. He ran inside. He didn't know where his sister and mother were. Tanks and what must have been personnel carriers drove through the fence and over the cherry trees and strawberry vines until the tracks were red with squashed fruit.

Then soldiers got out of the vehicles, and this part he told me when I was a kid. They threw grenades into the lake, and then watched to see the dead fish and toads float to the lake's surface. My father felt the explosions in his feet and legs as he ran from the window, as his mother called him, and they hid in the basement.

I could only piece together what happened next from Lil.

The soldiers entered the basement and shot wildly, bullets ricocheting off the concrete walls, making strange music as they shattered the light bulbs. One soldier pushed old Mrs. Simon behind the coal bin and she screamed. Lil heard a thump like a body falling.

Lil could hear what happened to Mrs. Simon but not see it. She was in the basement hiding in the chute under a pile of coal. Her mother had told her not to move until she called her. Lil knew now why her mother had sent her there, in that filthy place, to hide. She tried to cry without making sounds.

Dad does not know where his mother was when the soldiers entered the house.

Lil could hear the soldiers yelling on the stairs as they dragged her mother. She understood what they said in Russian but mostly it was cursing. Her mother talked in German almost as if she were talking to my dad, trying to get him to do something he didn't want to.

"Cunt. Fucking cunt." The soldiers' speech slurred and overlapped.

"Bitch." She heard the sound of ripping, spitting, and then the pounding started again.

Lil couldn't guess how many men there were, but more than two. Once, her mother made loud sounds, like an animal in pain, but then her voice subsided. After what seemed like a long time the men's voices went away. Helen called her daughter. She was at the stove, putting on a kettle with a shaking hand, her dress torn and cheek bruised, but she continued with meal preparations as if nothing had happened.

The soldiers came back for about a week and the same nothing happened over and over, at any time of day or night.

My father always refused to admit he remembered any of this. When pressed, he told me he remembered a drunken soldier backing over one of the last trees standing on the estate, a sapling, with his tank.

As the cab braked suddenly to make the long descent to Koropets, I wondered what unspoken traumas lay hidden in the boys' past, what stories they might tell their children, if they would be as tongue-tied as me and my father. Then the sun came out of the fog where Peter's orphanage lay nestled in the Carpathian foothills, like a scene on a postcard. We stopped to pick up the orphanage lawyer and the director, putting six people in a compact sedan designed for four. But we had only a few kilometres to the courthouse, which was a bare room with a large wire cage for accused criminals. The cage had a tiny ivy plant in an upper corner with one tendril moving optimistically across the top.

The judge, a red-faced man with a yellow shirt and frayed sports coat, entered with an attending secretary. We rose and he waved us back into our seats. In Ukrainian he announced the purpose of our case, to approve our adoption of Peter, and then suddenly began speaking English. "What is your name?"

Oleg had to nudge me out of my seat. I felt not only tired and hungry but completely confused by the judge's perfect English accent. I stood up and answered.

"Occupation?" he asked.

"Writer," I responded. Suddenly the air went dead and the judge reddened even more. I repeated *writer* in a loud monotone, thinking that the judge had not understood my pronunciation. The time stretched out and became rubber.

I saw myself as I imagined he must: an unemployable narcissist, born in the US, with a Canadian passport, divorced once, dependent on his new wife for money. This man with the perfect English accent and alcoholic's nose could bring his gavel down in careless judgment and we'd have nothing.

"My wife and I just want to have a family," I said out loud, deferentially.

Oleg spoke rapidly in Ukrainian and the judge's flush receded. The judge had paused at the edge of his English vocabulary, and Oleg rescued him from the cliff of his pride. That's what fixers were for.

The judge asked, through Oleg, the same questions I had in the morning. I gave the same answers, including my Ukrainian heritage story, but departing from the script, I also blurted out that it was very difficult to adopt healthy children at home.

"Don't say that," Oleg hissed, and did not translate my gaffe. I evaded his eyes and the judge's. Betsy looked pale.

"*Dyakuyu*," I said, *thank you*, and stopped talking. Oleg stared at me and Betsy did too. But at that moment I refused to try to justify adopting our sons any more. Relief flowed through me like mulled wine because I knew that the judge would say yes regardless; any further talk was just an empty formality. I knew what Betsy and I had paid to stand there. I knew how my family had paid with their bodies and with their ugly, fragmented stories, and how my grandmother stared grimly at a camera a few months before she died, in 1948, so I could stand here wordless and hopeful.

While waiting for the judge to make a decision we took turns sitting in his chair and photographing each other. Betsy moved her hands through her lush brown hair, pushing it back behind her ears for the picture in a gesture at once familiar to me and startling, her angular face and long fingers fierce with energy.

Oleg looked so comically grim in his simulation of the judiciary that I could imagine him presiding over some kangaroo court in Soviet times.

Finally the judge returned with his secretary. She handed him a two-page document covered with finely printed Ukrainian. He cleared his throat and read every word. According to Ukrainian law, we were approved as Peter's adoptive parents, but we had to wait thirty days to pick him up.

Thirty days. When the snow melts.

VI

At the airport Nikolai, Oleg, and Andrey shook our hands with bone-mangling sincerity. Betsy and I boarded the plane less than half awake. The first leg of our trip was on Ukraine International Airlines. They served *varenyky* and fried sausages for breakfast, but even better, you could order alcohol immediately, at 7:30 am.

I drank two glasses of red wine and then repositioned my pillow, writhing for half an hour in the small seat. The hell with sleep. I couldn't get over the feeling that the boys probably imagined we too were never coming back. That despair over abandonment must have been what my dad felt when his mother died. And I felt it too, trying to understand why Dad had kept running ever since the war, dragging my mother and sister and me, throughout the whole of my childhood, all over the Christly planet.

Dad said his sense of his own father, Cornelius, was "a blank." He never heard anything about him until arriving in Winnipeg as an orphan at the age of ten, and then his uncle Henry was the only one who spoke about Cornelius.

Henry was the drunkest, saddest, most atheistic and poetry-loving of Dad's maternal uncles. He'd been an adult when Cornelius was marched out of his home. Once near the end of his life Uncle Henry told me that Cornelius "had no sense at all, he was so *goddamn religious.*" But Henry couldn't tell the story. The one time he tried, he became so overwrought, crying and shouting, that he was incoherent. Much of his anger had to do with his own father, a religious maniac who kept his wife constantly pregnant and took pleasure in beating his children.

So I turned to my aunt Lil, who told me that, as a choir leader, Cornelius had led his youth group in a hymn, right in his own living room. They sang the religious words and they sang loudly. His neighbour reported the subversive activity. The authorities fabricated a charge of poisoning horses, a serious offence in an agricultural community. But everyone knew my grandfather was arrested at the end of 1937 because, as a Mennonite, he chose to sing only Christian words with his choir, not communist youth anthems. That was his crime against the state and his family. He never came back.

After the war my family assumed Cornelius had died somewhere up north in a labour camp, where work could set you free of your body. For Mennonites, not having his body was terrible, though. No matter how simple a church funeral was, the casket always stayed open so everyone could say goodbye. You couldn't say goodbye to a rumour, or a government document, or even a photograph.

In 1999 Lil got an official letter from Ukraine. The letter said that "with regard to the repressed Mierau, Cornelius," the former Soviet government had exonerated him of the charge that he was an enemy of the state. His exoneration was "due to lack of evidence."

The official letter also explained, in one sentence, how and when my grandfather died. He was shot on February 2, 1938, less than two months after his arrest, in the city of Zaporozhye, Ukraine. Lil showed me the duly notarized death certificate she received in 2000. She translated for me: the authorities on Lenin Avenue in Zaporozhye registered his execution in the Book of Acts of Death.

My grandfather made the choice not to run from the Soviet authorities, but he could not choose the vehicle of his death, a single bullet to his head. His widow Helen, my grandmother, chose to take her children and flee with the German army in 1943. She did not choose what happened to her later, outside Berlin when the Red Army arrived in their grimy, bloodstained vehicles. My dad, an infant when the authorities arrested his father, and a child when his mother took him to Germany, had no choice whatsoever.

My aunt Lil once told me that Henry had said to her: "If your dad, Corny, hadn't been so honest, he might have been able to escape. He could have hidden in other villages. Some Ukrainians took in Mennonites who had trouble."

Lil believed that her father was too committed to his faith to run away. Running would have been cowardly. She believed her uncle Henry was a godless man, and that his judgment was questionable.

But my grandfather's story was complicated, and hiding might or might not have worked. Mennonites were German-speaking pacifists and mostly farmers, and the ones who were left since the 1920s only small landholders. All Soviet citizens carried passports and my grandfather's said GERMAN on the lower right corner. The communist government saw all Mennonites as a national minority, a threat to the state. My family would have been surprised to know that they were seen as a threat, or that they were about to experience something which historians would later call the Great Terror.

In the only close-up photograph of Cornelius that exists, he appeared plain, determined. He wore a white shirt with a tie and a toothbrush moustache. I could understand why a man who looked like this could take a foolish risk. He believed in the next life, the one he was pushed into, with great faith. He believed in the pleasure of music. Part of me admired his pig-headed recklessness — a quality my father and I share, and which had landed Cornelius in the Book of Death. I thought of how Peter had pulled me and Betsy into him when we first met, a deep physical embrace of the Book of Life.

On the plane Betsy snored faintly beside me. I tucked the blanket around her shoulders and at last fell fitfully asleep before we reached Vienna, the wine's tannins jostling my brain, my body too long for the available space, the past a foreign country I could not escape.

VII

At home in Winnipeg our two cats, Alty and Ranger, had missed us: they rubbed against my legs and talked. Jeremy, when he was twelve, had picked out Alty at the humane society. When we brought her home she jumped on top of the bookcase where she could keep an eye on the room. Jeremy flipped through my Latin dictionary and found the word *altissimus* or "most high," and he named her Alty.

We called Ranger, who was black and white, the Trauma Cat. Her original owner, an old woman, had to move into a nursing home, and a social worker attempted to drive Ranger out of the basement ceiling using a broomstick without success. Finally a cat-loving neighbour managed to coax Ranger from the basement with food, and then persuaded Betsy to adopt her. Since then, Ranger had been deeply suspicious of almost everyone; I hoped she might take to the boys.

—

We started immediately to prepare the house for the boys' arrival in a month. Betsy painted their room and I drove around town picking up supplies and traveller's cheques, and running other errands. At Zellers we spent $800 on children's clothing in about half an hour. Then we bought bunk beds, a chest of drawers, a toy chest, and some toys, and worked together to put it all in place.

I had trouble sleeping. I read for a while and turned out the lights at eleven, fell asleep, and then woke every two hours after that, worrying. Under Ukrainian law, if any relative of the boys visited them at their orphanages during March, the adoption would be off. Our agency said they did not know of a single case of this ever happening and everything had gone according to plan. But I knew that you could get so close to something you longed for only to see it snatched away.

—

My grandmother Helen got so close to what she wanted for her family — safety, stability — and gambled all she had to get it. About a month after she was raped, a Red Army officer walked into her husband's house and demanded that she and the children come outside at once.

"You are Russian," the officer said to Helen, "we know because we found this." The soldiers had ransacked the Simon house, destroying or confiscating every scrap of food, stealing all the watches. The officer held a brown suitcase that came from the Soviet Union. Helen pretended not to understand, and asked in German for a translator. She knew the Red Army was combing every village in the eastern part of Germany for Russian citizens, always ready to send them to the Siberian Gulag.

"You see the hole here under this tree," the officer said. "If you don't confess the truth right now I will shoot all of you into it." And he took his revolver out of its holster. Helen's face was chalk-white but her hazel eyes dry and hard.

She looked at him without flinching and said in German, "You shoot us then." He lined up Helmut, my father, and Lil in the order of their heights and pointed the gun at one-year-old Helmut. But his knuckles were white on the trigger and his hand shook.

"You shoot us," Helen repeated in German, "I have nothing to confess." The officer re-holstered the gun.

"Get the hell out of here," he said, "I don't want to see you anymore."

As she told me this story, Lil was more shaken than when she'd told me about her mother's rape.

When I asked her why, she said, "I don't know, maybe because that was such a close call. He might have killed us." But Helen was a better gambler than her first husband had been, and they survived.

—

When my insomnia was at its worst I would get up, go to my office, and read. One night I picked up the diaries my father had lent me back in 2004 when I first tried writing about my childhood. They were a matching his and hers set in black and pink, and covered the years we'd lived in Africa. I hadn't touched the diaries since he'd lent them to me, but Betsy had, and told me how my father loved Africa, and how my mother cried and prayed and longed for home. Now I picked them up, driven to find a pattern, an explanation, a reason to anticipate a happy ending for my own second experiment with fatherhood. But I didn't learn much more than Betsy had.

—

"Are we still going to take an extra week to visit my father's village?" I asked Betsy when I was booking the return dates for the second trip to Ukraine. I'd already checked on the rail connections from Kyiv to the village, on having a translator, on what it would cost, and we had talked about this excursion into family roots even before our first trip.

"Yes, I think we should. But you know the boys won't remember this, and really it's more for you than for them," said Betsy, always more realistic than I. Tactfully, she didn't mention money. "Why don't we go to Ukraine a week early and visit the village on our own?"

"I want them to come with us. Of course they won't remember this trip. But we'll be able to remind them about it later, and show them pictures. It gives them another connection to my family."

"There's my family too," said Betsy, whose paternal grandparents spoke Polish and came from what is now western Ukraine, near where the boys were born.

"That's true. But your family doesn't know where exactly they came from. At least I have a place to start," I said.

Perhaps my obsession with family history was a form of narcissism. I was about to take children with whom I didn't even share a language on a tour of my family's violently disrupted past in Ukraine, when what they expected was to fly in an airplane to a house that contained cats, and toys, and parents, a house they'd seen in a single picture. What I hoped was that someday

Peter and Bohdan would understand how tightly entwined their story was with mine, and with my father's own troubled history.

VIII

At the end of March 2005, we went back to Ukraine to collect our sons. In the cab to Koropets to get Peter, I squeezed against Betsy in excitement and her eyes brimmed with happy tears.

We wanted to collect Peter first so that he could be part of picking up his younger brother. But first we had to pick up the boys' birth certificates in the village where they were born, and that delayed us by two hours. Betsy asked Oleg if we needed to buy candy for the orphanage kids. He did not respond. She asked again. Oleg said no, don't buy anything.

We arrived at Peter's orphanage just after noon during lunch hour — our timing was terrible. In the dark, cold hallway of Peter's dormitory, we were told to wait for lunch to finish. Shortly after one o'clock we were mobbed by a group of kids. Where was Peter?

There were two workers with the children. One of them stood in the middle of the hallway, facing us, and we heard sobbing from behind her. Peter was clutching her legs, crying on the floor. He didn't want to leave. But when Betsy picked him up he hugged her like a wrestler. Within a minute he was talking.

No one was ready for our arrival. I suspected that Oleg had not called ahead to let them know we were coming. Zaryana, Peter's favourite teacher, had to be summoned from her day off. The orphanage's lawyer didn't have the paperwork done and we spent more than an hour waiting for Oleg to come back from the lawyer's office.

Betsy insisted that we drive to the village of Koropets to buy candies for the children. Oleg now claimed that he had told us to buy them earlier. Shaking her head, Betsy drew her mouth tight and did not say anything. The fact was we couldn't have Peter's farewell party without candy and a translator. When we got back, Oleg was having an argument with one of the workers in Peter's classroom, who insisted that we should purchase a VCR for the kindergarten class. Later Oleg explained how he resolved this dispute. "I said you're a woman, I'm a man, I can't take your back-talk, your director has their donation and she will decide what to do with it."

In the classroom we handed out the candies. Peter helped us distribute them to his classmates, acting as if he'd bought them himself. A little boy kicked me between the legs and I sat hunched over on a bench for a few minutes. The party wrapped up with the kids singing to us, half-howling, Peter in the middle of them.

We went to the orphanage director's office with Peter. She told him to be good, and gave him a stuffed bear, chocolate, and a Ukrainian alphabet book. She said we must write letters, mail pictures, and send money through Western Union, just like the parents of Alla. Alla was the last child adopted from this orphanage. The director showed us a photo of the little girl in her new home in Florida. She was blonde and fragile-looking.

One more trip to Peter's dormitory. Zaryana was there to see him. She hugged him and cried, her makeup running. Then the other workers put Peter in four layers of clothing for the trip, purple tights, long underwear, jeans, snowpants. Oleg had been urging us to speed up ever since he'd finally gotten the paperwork from the lawyer. Betsy had to ask him twice to translate for her and he finally did so sullenly, persuading the workers to let Betsy take some of the clothes off Peter so he wouldn't roast in the taxi.

We took pictures of Peter's class outside on the driveway. He stood beside Zaryana and held her hand. In his other hand he clutched the black backpack we'd given him for his things.

Before we got in the cab, Peter pulled out Alla's picture from the backpack, claiming that he loved her, although he'd probably never met the girl. There was no time to think about how he'd gotten the picture because Oleg was trying to hustle us away as fast as possible. The haste was puzzling because we all knew we couldn't pick up Bohdan later than four o'clock, and it was already 3:30. It would take two hours just to drive to Ternopil. Betsy said to him that we didn't want to rush things that were important. He nodded absently.

———

The next day, when we arrived at Bohdan's orphanage, Peter called out loud hellos to the staff in the hallways and gave the director a bear hug. But when we reached Bohdan's group he looked stricken, like something was terribly wrong. He said a cursory hello to Bohdan, not the dramatic reunion we'd expected. Then he watched with me and Betsy as Bohdan's entire group sat in a circle on little plastic pails and urinated. Betsy wanted to ask some questions about toilet habits, but Oleg looked embarrassed. We'd asked him repeatedly if he could translate copies of the daily routines from both orphanages.

"You're the parents now," he said. He wouldn't translate. Then he said he had to leave to get the boys' Ukrainian passports. We were left with Andrey and the workers at the orphanage, none of whom spoke English. Peter barely talked but without Oleg we couldn't ask him what was wrong.

When Oleg returned he explained the mystery: Peter had been scared we would leave him behind at Bohdan's orphanage and take only Bohdan with us. Peter was now chattering away.

Oleg had bought candy and champagne, and we had a party. The children played with us for a while, but then they sat in their miniature desks, and Bohdan and Peter helped distribute candies. With Oleg translating, I tried to give a speech about how grateful we were to the orphanage staff for all their work. A few seconds in and I completely lost control of myself. My voice choked and snot streamed out of my nose. I couldn't cry in a dignified European way like Peter's teacher Zaryana. Betsy gave me a Ukrainian tissue with a mint scent. All the tissues had scents.

Everyone drank a glass of champagne, even Andrey. The children danced in a circle while they sang for us. Betsy and I joined the circle and we all danced. We took pictures. We shook hands with the caregivers. The one in charge had heavy white hair, a white smock like the other workers, and a martinet's manner. She talked to Oleg for a few minutes and then gave Bohdan a hug. Bohdan beamed with joy. One reason was that he was leaving his old shoes behind — they were too small and he loved his new runners and red backpack. Betsy had to strip a couple of clothing layers off Bohdan too.

Outside, Andrey opened the doors to the cab. Oleg was on his cell phone, talking to his new girlfriend. Peter got into the back seat. Betsy gave Bohdan a little nudge to move him in beside his brother. Instead, he sat down on the road. She picked him up. He pushed her away and began crying. She put him down. I talked to him in words he couldn't understand. What was wrong? Oleg was on the phone and wouldn't stop talking, so we could only guess that Bohdan was scared of the cab. He had likely never been in a car before; the kids were transported by ambulance when they came to an orphanage, and there were no field trips.

Bohdan broke into a full screaming fit. Oleg finished his phone call and informed us grandiosely that Bohdan did not want to ride in the taxi. But Peter demonstrated getting in and out a few times, and Bohdan finally allowed Betsy to place him inside. He was petrified but at least we were on the road again.

In the evening Oleg asked me for all four of our passports so he could buy us train tickets to Kyiv. He said he'd be back in half an hour. After two hours I began calling his cell. Busy. We were still jet-lagged and desperately wanted to sleep. Meanwhile the boys both refused to sleep. Peter got out of his bed, and when we made him lie down, he wailed. Bohdan screamed until he wore himself out, and then began rocking himself violently from one side of his bed to the other, a self-comforting behaviour I'd never seen before. Our fragments of Ukrainian did not console them.

Oleg's phone stayed busy almost until midnight, when he walked in the door. I was furious. But I decided screaming would do no good.

Early in the morning Andrey drove us to the Ternopil train station for our return to Kyiv. Oleg talked on his cell phone, ignoring us. We wanted him to ask for Andrey's address, and also to help us board the train. On our previous trip Oleg had looked after all such details. Now he shoved our tickets into my hands and I had no idea how to read them. Betsy and I were each pulling a large suitcase, carrying backpacks, and hanging on to our sons.

Conductors ran around, shouting, waving us in. Andrey shook our hands seriously, and seemed to ask Oleg if we were getting on the right car. Oleg kept talking on his cell. The part of the train we boarded did not have any sleeping compartments. I tried to tell Oleg, who finally turned in the narrow aisle and looked at the tickets. *This way*, he said, doing his imperious military wave, *follow me*. By the time we reached the end of the car the train was moving and we stepped through open air to get to the next car. I held Bohdan's hand tightly, and he started to cry.

We rushed through two more cars. By now I was worried that I'd wrenched Bohdan's arm from its socket. Our luggage was too wide for the aisles, but I'd stopped caring what or who we hit.

When we reached our compartment Oleg was about to scoot off. I'd been working up to this moment for days.

"Why didn't you look at our tickets before we boarded?" I said.

"I needed to speak with Nikolai." He looked irritated, face flushed, wanting to get away from me.

"You talked to him for more than ten minutes! We needed your help boarding the train. What the hell were you doing?" My voice was loud. I wished people around us could understand English, but Oleg did look embarrassed. He walked away, back stiff, clearly offended by my outburst.

In the first hour on the train, Peter crawled underneath the table in our compartment, exploring. Before I could grab him he laid his hand on the pipe that fed our steam radiator and began crying. He'd burnt the top of his right hand. After this he avoided the floor of the train.

At lunchtime I made multiple trips to the dining car to buy food for Betsy and the boys. Oleg helped me order. He was sulky, and I pretended that nothing had happened. Betsy was holding up well. After lunch, I asked if she was OK with the boys while I went back to the dining car and had a beer. I drank the beer quickly and started a second. Oleg sat with me. I bought him a beer, feeling like I should be conciliatory. But I didn't apologize or even mention chewing him out. What I really wanted, as I sipped my second half-litre of beer, was to hit him as hard as possible.

▬

We spent the next week in Kyiv as we'd expected, waiting for the Canadian embassy to process the boys' immigration paperwork and finalizing arrangements to visit my father's village. The downtown flat we rented combined frightening, filthy hallways with a comfortable interior. The landlord spoke broken English and told us two things: the boys must be *totally quiet*, and we must not break the washing machine. Peter and Bohdan spent a good part of each day screaming and throwing tantrums, but also gleefully laughing and calling to each other at high volume. They frequently made random adjustments to the washing machine, which kept working anyway. We took the precaution of unhooking and removing the TV and stereo from the living room where the boys slept on a sofa bed.

Betsy and I had to supervise Peter and Bohdan constantly. Their new experience of freedom made them fiercely willful. When it was mealtime, they refused to stop playing and hid inside a large chest of drawers; when we put them to bed at night, they cried; when we tried to brush Bohdan's teeth, he bawled. Bohdan also screamed when we bathed him; his previous life had included only bird-baths, not total immersion. Peter loved the bath and convinced Bohdan to at least tolerate it. In the morning they both sat on stools and watched with rapt attention as I shaved my head and face with a disposable razor and foam.

Mealtimes were free-fire zones, with food flying and landing in unlikely places as we tried to teach table manners. And either Betsy or I always stood because there were only three chairs at the kitchen table. The landlord refused our request for an additional chair.

Betsy and I used our few dozen words of Ukrainian to put the boys on time-outs, five minutes for Peter and three for Bohdan, to match their ages. During these time-outs they both had tantrums that involved kicking, arm-thrashing, foaming at the mouth, and energetic, bloodthirsty screaming.

Most mornings when I went to the café across the street for a western-style cappuccino, I felt like I was getting out of jail. Sometimes I took the boys with me for hot chocolate and to give Betsy a small break.

Almost every day we walked downhill to the Megamart for groceries. It was still fun to decipher the Cyrillic labels and explore the exotic mayonnaise flavours, the multifarious cookies, and the huge liquor section. The boys were somewhat quieted by the scale of the store. But only for five minutes. There were lockers for putting away personal items when you came in and the keys had large wooden fobs. Peter liked to work the keys in the locks and usually opened and closed numerous lockers while I struggled with getting bags of groceries into my backpack. He had a habit of pocketing things that he liked — stones, small toys, candies — as if he had to squirrel stuff away in case all his property was collectivized again, as it had been in the orphanage. Even though I took back two or three keys from him each time we left the Megamart, when we returned to our flat Peter inevitably had at least one key stuck in his coat pocket for a locker that wasn't ours. The next day I'd take that key back to the store. Peter secreted one key in his backpack that I didn't find until our return to Canada.

On sunny days we went to Shevchenko Park, about a twenty-minute walk. Peter and Bohdan played on the slides and swings. Neither of them had learned to swing in the orphanage, and we tried to teach them with limited success. They were both scared of the ponies that other kids their age were riding. Peter was thrilled by the battery-powered cars that you could rent, but we explained it was too soon for him. We had no idea how much he understood us yet. When the boys rushed around on the play structure I worried that they'd run off and get lost, and we wouldn't even be able to talk to anyone in the crowd.

Back in the apartment, between tantrums, they both loved to be held, cuddled, and kissed. Their skin was silky like Jeremy's bald head when he was born. At night, Betsy and I held each other and it was like the old days but even better.

IX

Once we'd finished with the adoption agency and Oleg, we had a new guide named Sasha, who came recommended by a Winnipegger with Ukrainian connections.

The first time we met him he pulled his blue Ford station wagon right onto the sidewalk in front of our apartment. He was tall and movie-star-handsome, in his mid-forties, with white hair and a soft voice. He'd been a scientist when he bought his American car. Then the Soviet Union collapsed and his monthly salary shrank to eight US dollars. He decided to learn English and become a tour guide. On the back seat of his car was a tattered copy of Antony Beevor's *The Fall of Berlin 1945*. Sasha noticed me looking at it. The book was more of a struggle to read in English than he really wanted, he said, and he sold it to me for ten US dollars.

Our first outing with Sasha as guide was to the war museum, which sat in a park under the two-hundred-metre-tall statue of the "mother of the motherland." Made from titanium and impressively hideous, the statue reminded me of the female monster in *Metropolis*. In the tunnel that ran underneath it we stared up at sculptures of giant citizens, soldiers, and other heroes conquering the Nazis, while a martial anthem played from hidden speakers. Nobody here could forget the Great Patriotic War just yet, the war that had followed the unmentionable period when the Soviets were Hitler's allies.

It was as if time stopped when Brezhnev built the museum in 1980; nothing was dated after that year. We walked around the first of the three floors with Sasha and the boys in tow. They were well-behaved at first, but soon got bored and Betsy had to take Peter and Bohdan aside to tell them not to run around, touch things, or yell. I asked Sasha to translate signs on display cases for me, all of which were in Russian only. The pictures of trenches and tanks straddling the flood plain of Kyiv seemed bizarre, as if I were looking at battlements outside Winnipeg.

In one of the Holocaust exhibits a group of American teenagers stared mesmerized at a film of the Babi Yar atrocity: naked bodies fell into a ravine, while menacing dogs and German soldiers stood at the edge. In the next room we saw a glove made of human skin from a concentration camp. Betsy took the boys outside to wait, while Sasha leaned against me and spoke in a confidential murmur.

"Many times, the Red Army got to the concentration camps before the Allies. They had the first chance to count victims. And in their arrogance, you know, they exaggerated. Not so many Jews died really. So you must think of this when you hear talk about six million dead." I said nothing, but it reminded me of my Mennonite relatives, their deeply ingrained anti-Semitism.

▬

The next morning I asked Sasha to take us to Babi Yar. There was little to see at the official Soviet monument built in 1976. The inscription did not mention the 34,000 Jews shot near here on September 29 and 30, 1941, by Germans and their Ukrainian collaborators; instead there was just a mechanical tribute to the Soviet "victims of fascism." The ravine slope here was not steep at the edge. Sasha didn't say so, but I knew from my reading that the real killing field was over a kilometre away, where the ravine does have the steep slopes on which you could easily imagine naked people forced down and shot by machine guns, then covered up by the next set of victims, in continuous layers of flesh and dirt.

Peter and Bohdan were happy to be outside, something rare for them in the orphanage, and they kept getting down on their knees and playing in the mud and grass. I tried to make them stand up, pointing at the mud on their pants. Betsy dusted them off, cheerful, then held their hands, swinging them on either side of her. The monuments meant nothing to them and we did not have Sasha try to explain.

The next day we went to the Kyiv zoo. Peter and Bohdan had hardly ever been off the grounds of their orphanages, and never for the purpose of fun, so they bounced in eye-popping excitement with us struggling to hold them back from jumping into bear pits and lion cages. We saw yaks, ponies, bison, geese, Chinese ducks, snakes, fish, monkeys, tigers, crocodiles, lizards — all in enclosures and cages laid out in an enormous, elaborately landscaped area. The Soviets had spent money on this place.

Sasha pointed out an amorous bear couple, rolling on their backs while they touched each other. "They make fore-wedding play," he said, "they have no sextual addeection." The unaddicted bears reminded him of the departure of his "beautiful wife" for America. He lowered his voice and confided to Betsy that "I had eight videotapes of pornography, and she find them before she leave." Sasha enjoyed talking about his messy love life.

During the day I used a calling card to telephone my father in Edmonton. I wanted him to look at a map for me, since I wasn't certain of our route for the next day. For once I had simple, practical questions. He was helpful, cheerful, enthusiastic. He asked me about the boys and I said they were exhausting but worth all the effort.

—

At dinnertime on April 8 Betsy and I boarded the train with Peter, Bohdan, and Sasha to see my father's village. It took ten hours from Kyiv to Zaporozhye, 600 kilometres to the southeast. The trip was awful. The train shook violently on corners, like a big dog after a bath, so Betsy and I had to hold the boys when they went to the toilet, trying to keep them from dropping in. They put their hands into everything, and their pants dragged all over the urine-soaked floor. We scrubbed them off as well as we could and hoped the orphanage had inured them to bacteria.

We had booked a sleeping compartment with four beds and when we put the boys into their new Zellers pajamas, they cried so loudly that we got a visit from a drunk in the next compartment. The shirtless man pulled open our door, fingered his belt and shouted unintelligibly, louder than Peter and Bohdan. He smelled of beer and sweat. We got Sasha, who tried calming him. Sasha claimed the man spoke in German. To me it sounded threatening and Slavic.

After the boys fell asleep, I bought a lukewarm Lvivske beer and talked to Sasha outside our sleeping compartment. Parenthood had been stressful and I looked forward to uninterrupted adult conversation. Sasha said he'd just read "this small book, maybe anti-Semitic a little bit," about how eighty percent of the Soviet government under Stalin had been Jewish, and how a czarist official was shot by a Jew in the Kyiv opera house, and that was what started the whole Bolshevik revolution.

My older Mennonite uncles and aunts had similar conspiracy theories. Even Lil observed that Hitler did some good things too, like making the trains run on time. Rather than remind her where those trains went, I just changed the subject.

Now Sasha pointed out that no Jews died in the September 11 attacks. That was because, he said, Israeli Mossad operatives warned them ahead of time. Osama bin Laden was a high-level agent run by Mossad in cooperation with the CIA.

I told him this was ridiculous anti-Semitic slander spread on the Internet. Many Jews died in the 9/11 attacks.

"The media," he said, "about fifty American and non-American Jews, they deciding what is on the news." So much for adult conversation. I excused myself and went to bed.

▬

The next morning we stumbled off the train at 5:30 am in Zaporozhye. All around us people marched like grim insects, silently, sometimes giving one of us a helpful push. Cars parked around us on the sidewalk as if we weren't really there. Sasha secured a taxi after some intense negotiating.

We drove down Lenin Avenue, the longest street in Europe according to our driver. At the western end we saw a statue of the great man pointing to the dam that thousands of construction workers lost their lives building. The city is named for the rapids that power the massive dam. Zaporozhye's concrete apartment blocks looked almost like pictures of Sarajevo under siege: broken windows, abandoned cars, graffiti, everything except bullet holes. Zaporozhye seemed like a good place for executions.

Our first stop before we left the city was a twenty-four-hour grocery where we bought gifts for people in the village. I walked with Sasha into the store past an armed guard and a sullen cashier. Sasha was a committed teetotaler and suggested not buying vodka or other alcohol, which was my first choice.

I was tired enough to take this advice and considered chocolates and candies. "If you feel very close, zat somevun is soulmate, you can always give money," said Sasha. I walked to the cashier with the gaudily wrapped packages, feeling certain booze would have made the better choice.

After passing many seedy apartment blocks and industrial scrap heaps, the cab driver took us on a four-lane highway out of town. For about half an hour the boys stayed quiet and Betsy and I just watched the scenery. Beyond the city you could see the green advance of spring.

Our driver recommended a detour to see a former Mennonite village other than Dad's. It was still only 7:00 am and we agreed. A little ways off the road was a broken-down brick building that had probably been a granary. A few scruffy dogs scratched themselves as if they were on Prozac and barking would be too much trouble. Betsy got out of the car briefly to take a picture, and we saw one perfectly preserved brick building with a chimney of elaborate masonry. Just outside the village we reached our destination: a flat stone monument to some Mennonite victims of the anarchist Makhno back in the 1920s. It had been recently placed by Canadians and engraved in Ukrainian and German with the names of the dead.

Bohdan had become whiny by the time we arrived at the monument. He ate part of an apple while making a hee-haw sound like a donkey with a sinus condition. After Betsy did her best to take a picture of the monument, which was too big to fit inside the viewfinder, she went over to Bohdan to pick up the pieces of apple he dropped on the ground in the tall grass. Then she tried picking him up. I was with Sasha, struggling with the German inscription on the monument, while he translated the Ukrainian for me. I heard Betsy make a whoofing sound like air escaping suddenly from a tire. Bohdan had kicked her in the lower chest, on the camera, which hung from her neck. She removed it from the case and tried advancing the film. Nothing. She tried taking a picture. Nothing.

For the first time Bohdan did not look cute and adorable to me. I wanted to smack him.

"Maybe Bohdan is filled with the spirit of the bandit Makhno," I said to Sasha, who did not laugh. Betsy did laugh, but we both knew the day had just gotten a lot longer.

We drove back to Zaporozhye. I didn't want to have come all this way only to leave without any visual record of the visit. Bohdan was crying and Sasha couldn't make him say why. We needed to be out of the car for a while. Since leaving the orphanage Bohdan had discovered a whole new emotional range, like someone who finds a pipe organ after only having a tin can with a stick. We didn't understand yet why he played the organ or how to make him stop.

Back on Lenin Avenue our driver took us to a mall with a buffet restaurant and a store that sold cameras and electronics. I changed US traveller's cheques into local currency. Transliterating my name into Ukrainian from my passport took them only about five minutes here and the whole process a relatively efficient half hour. During this time Bohdan kept lying down on the mall floor and refusing to get up, though he was quiet now. He was extremely tired, and it was only 8:30 am.

Betsy and Sasha and Peter had discovered that fresh batteries would not make the old camera go. Betsy bought a new one, an analog Olympus with a zoom lens. Within minutes I'd dropped it on the asphalt outside. But it still worked.

—

Back in the car Peter sat between me and Betsy when he wasn't trying to jump into the front seat, where Sasha spoke Russian to the taxi driver in a sleep-inducing murmur. Periodically Bohdan shrieked from the floor and again we had no idea why.

After thirty minutes that had felt like ninety we saw the sign for Nikolaipol. The houses were painted in fading pastels, many of them sagging from gravity's pull. Weird piles of straw and rotting lumber, twisted metal, and abandoned machines filled the yards. Old women bent over double with handleless brooms, dressed in rags and rubber boots. The road was gutted with deep potholes. There was only one new house under construction. The few houses that weren't crumbling victims of entropy stood in their solid brick with ornamental embellishments, built by Mennonites more than a century before their final exit; I recognized them from photographs in books about the area.

Upon Ukrainian independence the village was renamed Mikolaipol, the *n* changing to *m* in the transformation to Ukrainian. My aunt Lil still said Nikolaipol, the Russian version. Even though this region was Russian-speaking, the country had trouble with Ukrainian and Russian bilingualism. There was too much blood in the topsoil to imagine that two things could be true, or that a place could have two names. Lil couldn't imagine it either; she said Ukrainian was not really a language, just a form of Russian slang.

And another language lurked in the background here. The village had originally been named Nikolaifeld in German, after Czar Nicholas and one of those fields with six feet of rich topsoil. My Mennonite ancestors did the naming and also the farming, starting around 1800. They came from East Prussia, invited with thousands of others by the German-speaking Catherine the Great, who wanted to settle the Ukrainian steppes with experienced farmers: Lutherans, Catholics, Mennonites, and Jews.

Mennonites were allowed their own schools and were exempt from military service, as they wished, for a while. All they had to do was prosper, which they did, even as their privileges gradually eroded. But authority kept breaking down: the communist revolution, the vicious civil war of the 1920s, the Holodomor or Great Famine perpetrated by the Soviets on Ukrainian peasants in the early 1930s, and then various terror campaigns that culminated in world history's most murderous industrial restructuring, Stalin's collectivization of agriculture. World War II brought Mennonite life in Ukraine to an end. In 1943, 12,000 Mennonites fled Soviet Ukraine, many of them following the 21,000 who had already immigrated to Canada in the 1920s.

Looking out the taxi window the view resembled pictures I'd seen of small Mennonite villages in western Canada or Nebraska, the layout on a single street with the church, now converted into a granary, the most prominent building, a blacksmith's shop at the other end of the road. A rural Mennonite from a different century would instantly find his bearings here, and the place had a dream-like familiarity for me.

—

I was holding a photograph of the house taken by my aunt Lil when she visited here in the summer of 1983. In Lil's photo, apple trees bloomed in front of a white brick wall, hiding most of the structure. But I could see the decorative brickwork at one corner of the house's roofline, and it was like a puzzle piece that we tried matching with every brick house in the village. With the kids almost rioting in the cab we crawled in first gear through the single street, staring at every building.

By the time we reached the end of the village road, we still had not found the house in Lil's picture. We turned around and I was beginning to lose heart as we drove back at the same slow pace. Then, just off a T intersection Betsy saw an old brick column built around an electrical transformer. Lil had described just such a column "on the village road," now a muddy footpath. Diagonally across the street was the white house with the apple trees and brick trim. This was my grandfather's house, the place my father was born just before everything went to hell.

We got out of the car and Sasha introduced us to the current owners of the house, Vera and Ivan, in the driveway. They looked like aging potatoes that had squished sideways with the steady pressure of time. Their teeth stuck out at odd angles and their clothes were dirty. Vera talked about her grandson, who raised rabbits next door for their pelts and meat. He kept bees as well. Meanwhile, Peter climbed the fence, almost toppling the rotten wooden posts. When I explained that my father was born in their house, Vera and Ivan invited us to come in.

In the narrow kitchen, Vera served us milk curds with sugar, a thick and lumpy mixture that the boys loved and Betsy and I had trouble swallowing. Vera and Ivan said the house was ruined in the 1940s by collective farm workers and then rebuilt in the '50s. They told us they farmed beets and grain. We gave them the chocolates and candies I'd bought in Zaporozhye. They were indifferent and showed no reaction to my suggestion that their grandchildren might like the candies. I should have bought the vodka.

They offered to show me their house, and I nodded. Betsy, knowing how much this meant to me, said, "You go. We'll stay here and finish our milk."

The tiny house was laid out exactly as Lil had described back in Winnipeg, two bare bedrooms off the living room in front, the kitchen at the back. The living room was the last room they showed me, where my grandfather was arrested in the middle of a winter night in 1937, as the Black Maria waited outside. Harsh sunlight coming through the small, uncurtained windows illuminated how poor life had become for these farmers: no musical instruments leaned against the walls or rested on the worn furniture, no books sat on any surface. Throughout the entire tour, Sasha had kept up a running commentary in English, about his ruined marriage and ramshackle life. I had no chance to ask questions or even process what I was seeing.

Every detail in the house disappointed me, even the ones that I could have predicted, like the icon hung above the stove, so thoroughly un-Mennonite with its bloody Christ on a porcelain cross. Less predictable was Ivan's filthy white sweatshirt that said *Powder Puff Cheerleaders*. The boys kept calling from the kitchen and I could hear Betsy telling them not to touch the stove, not to spill their milk. Sasha talked and talked. I had expected to sit in reverent silence and weep in distress or bitterness. Instead I felt only irritated and tired, tired in my muscles and bones.

As we walked outside I noticed that there were fewer apple trees in front than in Lil's pictures. Sasha took photos with us in front of the house and at the side. Vera and Ivan played along with us funny tourists, posing for pictures, exclaiming in reluctance and amusement at the notion that they should have their pictures taken. Ivan smiled and threw out his hulking stomach. Vera smiled too, something my family did not ever do in the few surviving photographs from this place.

After spending more than an hour with Vera and Ivan, we went across the street to the site of my great-grandparents' former house, long since destroyed by fire. The current owner, a skinny woman of indeterminate age with a kerchief covering her head, said there were once four houses on the lot. Her house looked decrepit and she didn't ask us in. The garden in the front used to be beautiful, she said, though now it overflowed with miscellaneous junk. She could tell us nothing about my family, but was delighted with the gaudy chocolates I gave her.

———

We drove out of my father's village, packed back into the Volga taxi, hoping that Bohdan wouldn't have another maniacal screaming fit. The taxi driver suggested that we visit the museum on the island of Khortitsa. Betsy volunteered to stay outside with the boys while Sasha and I went inside.

The island of Khortitsa sits in the middle of the Dnieper River, just past the great hydro dam that first made Zaporozhye an industrial centre in 1932. My Mennonite ancestors farmed on this island and some of them got rich. The land was lush, and the river gave irrigation, transport, fish, life itself. Today the island looked uninhabited, covered by light brush, a convenient spot from which tourists could view the dam. The museum perched on top of the northernmost hill and was devoted almost entirely to Cossacks, with the exception of one scene from World War II, some Scythian armour, and a few pictures of eighteenth-century Zaporozhye, which was called Aleksandrovsk after one of the czars.

A single glass case housed the history of the German-speaking Mennonites who once lived here. The case held some self-published books from Manitoba with genealogical information, and a few scattered photographs. Nothing about how Mennonites invented the cream separator right in this area, or helped make Odessa a major port with their shipments of grain in the early nineteenth century, or ploughed up ancient Cossack burial grounds with Germanic industry.

This erasure of the Mennonite past seemed to fit with my mood. My ancestors were only here for 150 years. And in that time most of them didn't even learn the language, thinking it inferior to Russian and German just like Lil did. And in the end, they abandoned the fertile soil for other plains a world away, their work and their faith detachable from any national feeling, or loyalty to a particular time or place.

Back outside the museum Sasha and I found the boys playing with Betsy. We all took a walk along the river gorge in the spring sun. A southern breeze came off the fields of black soil that receded to the horizon in every direction. I could smell the earth warming as the season changed.

In the village Sasha had asked me if I wanted to take some soil as a souvenir. I did not. The black *chernozem* around Nikolaipol was never *my* soil. I'd never farmed, nor had my father. This rich black earth meant nothing to me other than a reminder that we all end up worm-eaten, improving the topsoil wherever we die. My ancestors had come for the soil. But they had no roots in it either. They came because their old home in East Prussia was too hot, breathing down their necks with the threat of military service and blood, and Catherine the Great gave them a chance to escape.

They left when there was too much blood on that black earth, when it began to seem too much like old Europe. Ukraine means "border" or "edge country," and my family was always on the edge, just like the Ukrainian people they tried to ignore, who lived all around them. Maybe a Canadian city on the plain would be better, a city framed by endless Doric columns of cloud and sky, air that never carried the smell of mass death, and wind that never stopped, blowing like a simoom or a Siberian gale every day.

X

In 1945, the border between East and West Germany that my dad and his family had to cross was hazy and open only sometimes, under the right circumstances. The bribery was not well organized. There was no one you could hire to put a fine burnish of legality over everything.

My dad's aunt Susan got across the border walking between horses at night with a sack draped over herself, "stiff-scared" according to Lil. In the wagon Maria Wiebe, Lil's grandmother, huddled under the hay, breathing out of a cardboard tube. Sometimes the border guards stuck pitchforks into carts going across the line, but not that night, at least not into her cart.

My father, Lil, their mother Helen, her baby Helmut, and her brother Dick and sister Mary all got off the train in the middle of a beet field near the British sector. It was the final darkness just before dawn. The moon lingered behind some cloud cover. Dick laid two bottles of vodka, an electric shaver he'd acquired when he was in the German army, and two wristwatches beside little Helmut in the baby carriage. Helen added her wedding band from Cornelius. Dick gave my father a bucket with a sponge to suck on and a handful of fresh strawberries, which must have been hard to come by.

Dick wasn't sure exactly what direction to go in, except that they must move west. Mary, whose brain was garbled by childhood meningitis, lost one of her galoshes in the muddy beet field, and she went down on her knees looking for it. Just then the moon came partly out from behind the clouds. There was gunfire. The Russian border guards had seen them.

The Russians were boys, barely nineteen. They pointed their rifles at the family and said, over and over, *"Uhr, Uhr,"* wristwatch. Dick handed them the two watches from the baby carriage. The soldiers still wouldn't let the family go, so Dick pulled the vodka bottles out of the carriage. Helmut made a low moaning noise since the bottles had held him in place like glass cushions. One of the Russians looked into the carriage and saw Dick's shaver.

"What the hell is this? Does it shoot?"

"*Nein*," said Dick, after pretending not to understand their Russian for a minute. "It makes you look good. You can shave your face smooth like this tree bark." He mimed a shaving motion on his face and then ran his hand over the tree.

They nodded to each other and one of them pocketed the shaver and said, "OK, you can go. But you leave the girl here with us." He pointed at Lil, who was thirteen.

"Take this instead," Helen said, handing them her wedding ring from the carriage. Little Helmut started to cry the way babies do when they are about to get very loud. Looking nervously back for his commanding officer, the older boy said, "Go fast, all of you."

It was still mostly dark even with one edge of the moon showing. They walked quickly away only to be stopped a few minutes later by another group of border guards. These were older.

"The girl stays here and you can all go," they said. Helen said, "No. We have nothing for you." The guards, distracted by another group emerging from the mud, fired their guns into the air. Like a giant in the semi-darkness, Dick ferried them across the stream, first Lil, then Mary, then my father, and finally the baby carriage above his head as Helmut squalled.

When he put Helen down on the other side he knelt beside the stream, panting, cupping water into his mouth.

Helen said, "We made it so far — you can't drink that water — what if you get shot?"

"Shut up, I'm thirsty," said Dick. Then some English-speaking soldiers appeared and gave them baloney sandwiches, something new. They had reached the west.

XI

On our last Sunday evening before going home to Canada we went to the Kyiv circus, which is permanently housed in a small domed building at Victory Square. We sat near the front. A woman in a tight blue dress descended from a large staircase as lights flashed around her. Peter gasped and exclaimed; he had never seen so many lights. The band played from a balcony while the woman sang some kind of Broadway-disco *welcome to the circus* song. The performers trouped around the ring in garish costumes, waving and preening at the audience.

It occurred to me that my dad had never taken me to the circus, nor did I ever take Jeremy. This was my chance to break the mold.

For Peter the bears were the climax of the show's first half. His changeable grey-green eyes bulged out of his head like telephoto lenses as the mangy bears rolled in steel cages, rode scooters and motorcycles, danced, turned cartwheels, and — most impressively — drove cars. A man and woman in flowing velveteen paraded around with them as if they were responsible for the sheer cleverness of these animals. They could well be, I thought, wondering what weird, sadistic training would make bears turn cartwheels and drive vehicles.

Bohdan's favourite act was a group of masked acrobats in Spider-Man outfits decorated with ultraviolet lights. At the intermission Sasha said that Bohdan's fascination with these demonic costumes showed his affinity with the occult. But Sasha still gave the boys almonds to crack, which Peter did with his shoe on the concrete floor. Bohdan handed his to Peter for the same treatment. Then as the second half began Bohdan went crazy — crying and crumpling to the floor.

Betsy leaned across and said, "Why don't I get Sasha to take us back to the hotel and you can stay here with Peter."

"Sure," I said, and she nodded.

Peter and I settled in happily to watch the reptile charmer who had just come to centre stage. He was a bearded man with a feathered hat and an ornately upholstered vest. Young women in harem costumes stood on the edge of the ring and, accompanied by crashing cymbals, he draped cream-coloured snakes over their upturned arms.

Then six teenage boys ran out into the ring and let loose seven squirming crocodiles in a range of sizes from smaller than a dog to larger than a man. Some were distressingly active, scampering around the ring. Peter's legs twitched with excitement.

The charmer walked with great dignity, pointing dramatically at one crocodile after another, magically freezing each into a state of hypnosis. One kept moving around, and the charmer had to return to freeze him a few times. Peter clapped and laughed, repeating "*Dihveetsya, dihveetsya,*" *look, look!* as the charmer hung two of the crocs on the edge of the ring within snapping distance of the audience in the front row.

In his excitement, Peter grabbed my hand, and I had a sudden bizarre image of myself in the parade as the ringmaster, controlling the circus, Sasha and Oleg dressed as clowns, Betsy a showgirl dressed in sheeny fabric, strong and acrobatic, an athlete.

But then my father entered with his beard and suit, dressed like the crocodile charmer, holding a violin. As he fiddled and changed tunes at lightning speed we all began moving at his command, just as we had when I was a kid. Then he tripped over a crocodile, his playing faltered, and I felt helpless rage at his restless energy, his deliberate amnesia, his aloofness. But then Peter, Bohdan, and Jeremy came on stage in the gaudy vests and white shirts of the charmer's assistants. And I remembered that I was holding the microphone, that I was the ringmaster. And gratefully, I squeezed Peter's hand.

———

Nikolai drove us to the Kyiv airport just after 4:30 in the morning. We arrived in Toronto on April 12, cranky and exhausted from a fifteen-hour flight during which the boys had not slept at all. We had a ten-hour layover in Toronto.

Betsy took a much-needed break from the family by reading *People* magazine. The boys and I sat at a window to watch the airplanes. Peter and Bohdan kept wandering away. I said, "Boys, you have to stay here," and kept dragging them back when they didn't. The third time, they shouted at me.

"*Caca! Pisca! Caca! Pisca!*" said Peter.

"*Caca! Pisca! Caca! Pisca!*" said Bohdan. Something scatological, I assumed. That's it, I thought, we won't be talking pidgin-Ukrainian to the boys anymore.

"From now on, Mom and I will talk English to you."

"*Nee likey*," said Bohdan, his abbreviation for *I don't like that.*

———

The boys and I finally fell asleep just minutes before our plane left for Winnipeg. Betsy took a picture of us, me stretched out on the floor using *The Fall of Berlin* for a pillow, and the boys slumped over the steel armrests of a bench like the hypnotized crocs at the circus. Then when we boarded the plane the boys both screamed without stopping. They refused to wear their seatbelts and fought like rabid dogs while the flight crew helped us pin them to their chairs and secured their belts, all while people filed onto the plane staring at us. They screamed all the way up to 30,000 feet in the air. They woke up and yelled again for the descent into Winnipeg, where spring had miraculously arrived. April 13, 2005: not a speck of snow on the ground. In the early morning darkness we stumbled out of the cab and a warm breeze stirred the budding elm trees on our block.

DETACHMENT

I

On our first day back in Canada, I woke to bangs and giggles from the boys' bedroom. Betsy's eyes snapped open. I put my arms around her and pretended not to hear anything. Jet lag rattled through my brain like a tornado. A body thudded onto the floor.

"We have to get up," said Betsy, and we both willed ourselves upright and into the boys' bedroom. Peter lay on the floor as if he'd been transformed into Kafka's insect, but he was grinning, his absurdly long eyelashes radiating energy. Bohdan jumped on his lower bunk bed trampoline-style, just low enough not to bang his head, looking mischievous and worried at the same time.

"Good morning, *molodets*, welcome to Canada," Betsy said. She smiled and pulled up the blinds. Spring sunshine poured in from the southern exposure. Bohdan yanked open the chest of drawers and began throwing his new clothes over his shoulder until I stopped him. His body burned with energy and, I imagined, fear. But he had no English words to tell me that yet.

Peter learned the English alphabet in the afternoon of that first day in Canada. Betsy wrote it out and he copied it over and over on a small chalkboard. His failure to learn the Cyrillic alphabet in his orphanage was not the result of a learning disability. We have a picture of him from his second day in our house, holding the chalkboard with his name written three times, smiling through what was left of his baby fat and starch-laden diet, looking almost crazy with happiness.

—

Somewhere in those first few days I called my parents in Edmonton. Knowing they would be curious, but unlikely to call me first, I told them how happy the boys were, putting their arms around each other, sitting on our laps when we read to them, pulling string toys in front of the cats — who were indifferent. Mom asked, as she always did, if Betsy was very busy at work; I explained that Betsy was on parental leave for six months to spend time with Peter and Bohdan. Then I put the boys on the telephone. Bohdan didn't understand that he needed to talk — he just held the receiver at arm's length and stared. Peter jabbered with enthusiasm for a minute or two, but Dad, even though he remembered some Russian, could not understand Peter's accent.

When asked how soon they could come to Winnipeg to see his new grandchildren, my Dad, who has never liked pinning down dates, said maybe they'd drive in June. I was disappointed it couldn't be sooner, but didn't say so.

—

On the weekend Jeremy came over to meet his brothers. I hadn't seen much of him for a while — he'd stopped spending the night at my house a few years back. He was skinny and awkward-limbed with a pasty complexion that I assumed came from staying up at night playing his Xbox.

When the door swung open I could smell the premature spring. We gave Jeremy his souvenir, a T-shirt, and introduced him to the boys. They shook hands solemnly as they'd been taught. He didn't hug them, which did not surprise me. I hadn't hugged him since he was eight or nine. My own father hugged me for the first time that I could remember when I was in middle age, and his hugs were stiff and awkward, like a board, just like mine.

We had asked Jeremy over so we could take a family photograph. Betsy set the camera to self-time and rushed back before the flash. In the photo Peter and Bohdan perch on my lap in the middle, with Betsy to my right and Jeremy left. My sons and I wear our garish Orange Revolution T-shirts and Betsy has a matching orange toque and scarf. All of us smile except Peter and Bohdan, who stare, deadly serious, straight at the camera. They look scared.

—

That first month Bohdan entertained us every night at dinner with the same routine. He had to wear a bib because he was still learning about cutlery and how to sit up at a big table. Early in the meal, before the bib was covered with food particles, he'd flip it over his head and grin through his baby-fat cheeks. Then he said *babushka, babushka,* until we would laugh. It was one of the last Ukrainian words he spoke, since both he and Peter had stopped speaking their first language to each other the minute our plane landed in Winnipeg.

The boys grew almost an inch every thirty days in those first few months. We spent a lot of time watching them eat, at meals and at snacktime. They were continuously hungry and our grocery bills tripled.

In April on my first expedition to the giant Superstore in the west end, the aisles seemed too wide and the choices obscenely abundant. Part of me remained in the Megamart in Kyiv, cringing from contact with the shoppers who flowed around me like water, wafting the scents of cheap perfume, cigarettes and liquor, musky bodies and cheese, bread and sausage. And so this big box store was a shock: I never came close to anyone, I couldn't smell anything except cleaning supplies, and everything was arranged as illogically as possible, to drain digits from my bank card along with hours from my day.

For the most part, Betsy stayed home with the boys. She had a very clear idea of how she wanted to parent and manage the household with its new members. Before we had them, we'd talked about raising kids in general terms, and agreed easily that we would stay organized, continue to have date nights, be egalitarian with the chores and loving with the boys: there would be, for example, no corporal punishment. While Betsy was on leave I would focus on my writing. But I at least had utterly failed to picture how any of this would work out in reality.

In my third-floor office, with the door closed, I tried to explore the connections between my father's terrible childhood and the adoption of my new sons, often just staring at the blank screen or spending hours reading sports news online. Downstairs Peter and Bohdan played with Betsy and each other, squealing with joy in their new profusion of brotherly togetherness, and protein, and love from a mother who was patient, calm, and not locked away in a room they weren't allowed to enter.

In our weekly phone calls, Dad was still vague on their plans for coming to Winnipeg. I put the boys on the line again, this time with the speaker phone, and Mom complained that their accent was so heavy she couldn't understand what they said. Edmonton was far away. Knowing his reluctance to talk about the past, I avoided asking Dad the questions that preoccupied me.

At mealtimes I was shocked at how easily Betsy spoke to the boys, how she anticipated what they wanted, how gently she corrected them. Even when I was at the table my mind lived inside my fragmentary manuscript, imagining my father's childhood. Betsy found this frustrating, and I noticed that she sometimes used the same tone with me that she did with the boys when they misbehaved. The fact that after two years I had virtually no income from my writing filled me with a gnawing insecurity. Meanwhile back in my office I watched World War II movies, read books about Soviet history, read every scrap about NBA basketball that I could find on the Internet, and wrote very little.

—

In May we bought the boys bicycles, a bright yellow one for Bohdan, tiny, and a red one for Peter, slightly bigger. Both bikes had training wheels. We unloaded them from the car onto the sidewalk and Betsy adjusted the helmets. I lifted the boys onto their new bikes. Peter immediately got off and began studying the wheel assembly and the steering column, gesturing with his hands like an Italian, saying "bicycle" over and over. I used my hands to show him how to move the bike pedals, then loaded him back on, feeling how solid he was. As his legs began moving with the pedals, I touched them and said "push." He did some tentative pedalling and I let go of the bike. He was moving, on his own steam, and he smiled. I stepped back panting, feeling proud of him.

Then I turned to Bohdan, who had not moved since Peter began riding. Bohdan had the same beatific expression on his face as Peter did when he was in motion, but Bohdan was making no attempt to move. Betsy held one of his legs and demonstrated a pedal stroke. Bohdan continued to smile and looked either straight ahead, without any pressure on the pedals, or down at the bright yellow paint of his bike.

Meanwhile Peter had driven into our neighbour's hedge and fallen off his bike in awkward slow motion. He didn't respond to this even as an inconvenience, getting up quickly, not dusting off or noticing the gash in his pants, but just getting back on the bike and pedalling again.

I came up to Bohdan and said, "Push?" and he nodded hard. "Yes," he said, the first time he hadn't said "*tak*" for the affirmative, one of his last Ukrainian words. I pushed, holding him, noticing that he had the same stocky build as his brother, and with a long waist and big chest. I'd always wanted to be big-chested like my maternal grandfather, and now I had a son with that build.

With me pushing him we travelled the length of the block, but he still wouldn't pedal his bike. I called Betsy and she looked at him for a minute as he gazed down at his bike, lost in admiration. "Get the camera," I said, and she ran into the house.

—

My first time alone with the boys was just a few hours long, a morning. I put on a Sesame Street video; Betsy and I'd agreed on the acceptability of some educational TV. Peter kept rubbing against me from the side, thrusting his body into any open space where he could reach the buttons on the TV equipment. I said no and finally placed him on the couch. When I hit play both of the boys rushed the screen, knocking the glass with their fists, roaring each other's names and shoving. I picked them up one at a time and plunked them down on the couch.

"You can watch now. Just watch."

Peter pointed at the screen and laughed at Cookie Monster. Bohdan stood and they both attacked the screen again.

"Boys, sit down." They ignored me. I put them back on the couch. Their skin smelled like milk, as if they'd just dropped out of the baby factory, and that innocent smell calmed me.

I began work in the next room, then heard them arguing about something and running around the room. When I went back they were both climbing onto the TV stand. I grabbed their wrists and pulled them in front of me so my face and my breath were right in their faces and shouted. Bohdan stared right back at me, but Peter's eyes darted all over the room.

I knew I'd frightened them. I'd frightened myself too. They wailed and their doll-like eyelashes got dewy. I felt unsure of myself in a way I'd never experienced with Jeremy, who had been docile at their age. These kids seemed more like wild dogs who needed me to establish dominance over the pack, not exactly my strong suit.

Near the end of her parental leave, Betsy spent a few days at her office to prepare for the upcoming school year. On Friday I took Peter and Bohdan on the bus to meet Betsy at the university. I sat between them, directly behind a kid in full Sex Pistols regalia, sprouting body piercings and an aggressively purple mohawk that stood a full four inches above his head. The boys pointed at him and giggled and the mohawked kid ignored us.

"My hair. . ." Bohdan didn't have much vocabulary yet, and when he couldn't express something he just made sounds and hand motions like Harpo Marx. I'd recently taken them to see *Duck Soup*.

"Yes, we'll talk to Mom about having your hair like that. It's called a mohawk." I was scared that Bohdan would actually remember this conversation but fortunately he was distracted by a blind man entering the bus with his dog. I had to explain why we couldn't pet a working dog. Bohdan loved animals.

Peter kept trying to cross his legs but he had trouble getting one leg all the way over the other, as though he didn't quite have the energy to move his leg where he wanted. It was like watching Gumby with the stop-motion badly timed.

Betsy was waiting for us at the main university stop, backpack on, reading a novel. The boys saw her before I did and charged out of the front door of the bus, banging into the passengers waiting to board. I followed as quickly as was politely possible. Peter ran toward Betsy, but after two awkwardly large steps he face-planted on the concrete just in front of her.

"Are you OK?" she said, kneeling down. Bohdan and I arrived a moment later. Peter had a scrape on his chin that he wouldn't acknowledge. He was fine.

That first summer with the boys none of the people we knew who spoke Ukrainian were around. We wanted the boys to learn English, but also to keep their first language. It was especially important to me because I had lost German, my only language until age two.

After inquiring with friends, we enrolled the boys in nursery school at Holy Trinity Orthodox Ukrainian Cathedral on Main Street. They spent two mornings there every week in June and July. I drove them and picked them up; on the way we listened to a compilation of children's music that Betsy's brother Andrew had put together for them as a gift. Peter sang along very loudly, especially to the Raffi tunes, and Bohdan made tuneless word-sounds that were neither English nor Ukrainian.

I walked them into the cathedral basement, which reminded me of an older Mennonite church, built by volunteer labour, with linoleum floors and the feeling of a huge rec room. The boys' teacher was a recent Ukrainian immigrant named Halyna. They were always delighted to see her but ignored the other kids and even each other, preferring to play alone. Sometimes Bohdan tried to play with Peter, but Peter was rarely interested. Their favourite toys were kid-sized cars that they self-propelled around the big open area.

Some days I would stay and have tea with the older women who ran many of the programs at the cathedral. They asked me where the boys came from in Ukraine, why we went there to adopt children, did I know they sold perogy every third Saturday in the basement? And they offered to help with keeping up the boys' language, although such help would involve me driving for hours into the Kildonans.

On one of the last days of the program, one of the women said to me, "Your boys are so good-looking, and that's an asset in life, you know." I was proud and strangely reassured. It was hard to know how the boys looked to other people; mostly I worried that people thought my kids were out of control, and that it reflected badly on me.

Every time I dropped them off for the morning I felt tremendously relieved and also guilty that I couldn't imagine having my own kids with me for more than a few hours at a stretch. They exhausted me. That couldn't be normal. Betsy had also talked about her exhaustion dealing with the boys' tremendous energy level, but even with her full-time job she spent more time with them than I did.

—

For the graduation ceremony from Ukrainian kindergarten, the boys needed to wear traditional white blouses with embroidery up the middle and at their wrists. So I took them to a store on Selkirk Avenue nearby that the ladies at the church had mentioned.

The tiny store contained a bewildering variety of goods from Ukraine, including trident flags of every size, imported candies, DVDs, frozen perogies, wooden nesting dolls, and Ukrainian books. Peter and Bohdan charged in opposite directions with all the manic energy of Thing One and Thing Two in *The Cat and the Hat.* They touched and grabbed at every item within reach. For a moment I stood watching with embarrassed fascination, half-expecting them to begin eating the flags and dolls that they touched, so blatantly sensual was their activity.

But my limbs thawed when they reached the shipping area in the back, which had a DIY station with bare utility knives and a tabletop slicer. Bohdan clutched the slicer handle like a Jacobin. With no effort at all I could imagine one of his surprisingly thick boyish fingers severed and twitching on the slicer. Or one of Peter's: he was trying to body-block his brother off the machine.

"Peter and Bohdan, come here!" They didn't respond and no one in the store did either. In three steps I snatched them away from the slicer, clutching each of them by their polo shirt collars, which worked as convenient handles.

"Hold my hands, both of you." Bohdan giggled. Peter recognized the pressure of my hand around his as coercive. He blinked rapidly but did not cry. We walked to the counter where an unshaven man with thick arms unsmilingly handed me two blouses in the boys' sizes. While Peter tried one on I held Bohdan wedged in front of me, wrapping my legs around him so he couldn't budge. Then they traded places, Bohdan in the change room, Peter between my legs, but Peter broke free one more time, colliding with other customers who didn't seem in the least rattled. Maybe I'm too uptight, I thought, it's a different culture.

In the car, though, I was breathing hard and still seeing the chaos, my inability to control them or keep them safe.

"You can't behave like that in a store," I barked, volume muffled by my shallow breaths. "You've got to calm down." They both nodded at me, surprised at how upset I was, and we drove home in silence.

—

That night, wanting a much-needed shower, it took longer than usual for the water to warm up. Our house had antiquated plumbing and more demand placed on it lately, so I waited some more, but the water stayed lukewarm.

In the basement I discovered the pilot light was out on the hot water heater. Hoping we wouldn't have to buy a new heater, I got on my knees, reset the control and struck a match, and the gas caught fire again.

The next night the pilot light was out once more. Betsy was suspicious. Peter and Bohdan played in the basement while Betsy prepared dinner, and had strict instructions to stay in a carpeted area far from the tools, the furnace, and the water heater.

In the morning Betsy asked Peter if he'd touched the water heater. He said no, and I thought he probably didn't understand what she was saying. But at lunchtime when I came down to call them they were both hunkered near the water heater and Peter had his hand on the dial.

"What are you doing, Peter?"

"Nothing," he said, without removing his hand from the knob. Betsy and I cross-examined him for half an hour upstairs. He looked straight at us with his beautiful grey eyes wide open and even though we assured him we wouldn't be mad, he refused to admit a thing. We moved the toys back upstairs.

▬

Often the boys ran up to my office to call me to dinner, knocking at the door and then almost knocking me over, giving me burly hugs like miniature rugby players. Before we had kids Betsy and I used to chat over dinner, about politics, our day, our plans. Now Peter talked so much we couldn't get a word in edgewise. He talked about trucks and vehicles and traffic signals, words delivered at unnatural speed. I kept my head down under the barrage of words and ate rapidly. Betsy asked the boys questions about what they were doing. She did not seem as bothered by their limited vocabulary. I loved them, but did not know what to say to them, so when I talked at all it was mostly to Betsy, and usually about subjects they could not understand. Peter started talking exclusively to her when he figured out that I didn't listen. When he addressed me he'd say "Dad" three or four times, trying to recall my mind from my computer's spinning hard disk upstairs.

On Sunday nights I called my parents and talked to them about sports and politics. My mother, in the early stages of dementia, often repeated stories within one conversation, but she still knew the names of politicians and athletes. Dad still loved the Lakers. They didn't ask to speak to the boys and I didn't offer to put them on the phone, and I often hung up feeling that we had left the most important things unsaid.

II

Betsy's mother Molly died that May in Illinois, though Betsy said Molly had actually died five years earlier. Already suffering from Alzheimer's, she'd had a massive stroke in 2000 that damaged her brain so badly she had to live in a nursing home. She was sixty-three.

The one time I saw her there it was dinnertime in the dementia ward. The residents stared quietly at their trays of food or at the television as if locked in a terrible and futile state of concentration. The air was fetid. Many let their heads loll sideways.

Molly's eyes were dead. She didn't recognize Betsy although at the sound of her voice Molly stirred slightly, maybe by accident. Molly had been a funny, gregarious woman who invited strangers she met at the grocery store to join family dinners. Here she was wearing diapers. Betsy suspected the dark lines under her nails were fecal matter. Fred, Betsy's dad, constantly battled the home's administrators to make sure Molly's diaper was changed more often.

Molly's health continued to decline and then she lost the ability to swallow food. Assured by the doctors that Molly had a few more days, Fred came to Winnipeg to meet his new grandsons. He spent one day with us. Then we heard his cell phone ring at 2:30 am, and found the next morning that he had left for Illinois without waking us to say goodbye. In the morning Bohdan asked me why Poppy had to leave.

"Grandma Molly died last night. Poppy had to go home."

"Will Poppy die?" said Peter.

"No, not now, Peter," I said. "He's doing fine." This wasn't strictly true. He had a heart condition and bladder cancer. But Fred was still active and his mind sharp.

We decided to rent a van rather than fly from Winnipeg to Champaign for the memorial service; it would be cheaper and we'd see if the boys would do any better on the road now that they were more settled.

I was nervous driving such a large vehicle and made a wrong turn at the end of our block.

"Maurice, we have to go south," said Betsy, in a neutral tone.

"Yeah, I know," I snapped, edgy because I'd had to rush my morning coffee.

"You're driving us north."

"Yeah. OK. Do you want to drive?" I took a right turn at random, my voice going up in pitch.

"No. No, I don't." Betsy stayed neutral, which she knew drove me crazy.

The boys were great on the road. For hours they stared at the barren landscape of North Dakota — the American steppes — as if mesmerized, while they listened to Raffi and Fred Penner on their headphones. We didn't make bathroom breaks any more often than we used to on our own.

Then somewhere in western Minnesota Bohdan said he had to go to the toilet *now*. His face scrunched up like a gargoyle, and he emitted a very bad smell. I turned off the highway into a rest stop within a few miles. On the long driveway going in there was a pop from one of the tires and the van sagged at the back left. We limped to the parking area and emerged from the air-conditioned van into the blazing summer heat.

I hate changing tires and always worry I'll crush myself under a vehicle by placing the jack in a dangerous position. A friendly midwesterner in golf clothes saw me fumbling ineptly with the spare and offered to help me. He was an angel of competence and we put the spare tire on the van in a few minutes.

Meanwhile Bohdan had been to the bathroom with Betsy and Peter. Turned out he had no business to do there.

"You have to say what you want," said Betsy, irritated.

"He did. Just without telling you," I said. We had to buy a new tire because we'd driven over a razor blade. We got back into the van sweaty and annoyed but Bohdan looked like a boy chorister and it was hard to stay angry with him.

During the last three hours of the trip south, I kept asking Betsy to watch the signs for me on the eight-lane, perfectly straight Interstate 90 that went directly to our destination. I had a history of exiting this highway without intending to, and leading us into rush-hour traffic just outside Chicago, three hours off course.

"Why can't you read the signs yourself?" asked Betsy the fifth or sixth time I demanded confirmation that we were on the right highway.

"I have trouble paying attention to everything going on at once. The boys in the car, the other vehicles going by faster than I'm used to in Canada, talking to you . . . Studies show men can't deal with multiple inputs as well as women, you know."

"Oh, bullshit, Maurice. The signs are gigantic."

She turned around to look at Bohdan in his car seat, singing at high volume with his CD player. "Are you having fun, baby?" she said to him, squeezing his knee. He smiled and I felt an absurd twinge of jealousy.

"Don't you think I'm doing better than before? We're not in Schaumburg, delayed for three hours," I said earnestly to Betsy, back to the fraught subject of my driving.

"Yes," she said, voice heavy with irony, "you're doing so much better. You keep asking me to read the road signs, like you always do."

"Don't you think people can change?"

"No, I don't think people change very much."

I kept a dignified silence. My belief in self-reform was at a level of passion that Oprah herself would have admired. I almost missed the next turn, trying to figure out what was making me so angry.

———

The Mennonite funerals that were part of my childhood always had an open casket, so everyone could view the peaceful deceased in their state of heavenly bliss, accompanied by ponderous, beautiful hymns and ponderous, ugly sermons. After the formal ceremony, the reception always took place in the church basement.

Molly's memorial, at a country club, was what my parents would call a reception. There was no ceremony, no body, no casket, nothing to *view*. People milled around with cocktails and tiny bits of food. The men wore closely-fitted golf clothes and the women used a lot of hair products and makeup. Betsy never wears makeup.

A computer displayed photographs of Molly at different stages of her life, a boisterous woman converted into a digital museum of eternal silence. When it was finished we were all ushered outside for a photograph, and then it was over.

That evening we were to join the rest of the family at a restaurant in franchise-land near the edge of town. On the drive there, Peter talked non-stop. "Look how high the lights are. And there's four of them! See the arrow? Why does that car have so bright lights?" Bohdan said nothing, which was normal when Peter did his machine gun chattering routine.

"If you want to change lanes, you'll have to be aggressive," said Betsy.

"Changing lanes with all this traffic weaving around makes me nervous."

"Maurice, it's a small town."

I said nothing, but something beyond her nagging bothered me.

The waiter at the nominally Italian restaurant insisted that we call him Todd, and bragged about how they served olive oil instead of butter. We ordered pizza for the boys, which they'd never had before, and they didn't like it. But both of them sat happily on the laps of uncles and aunts they'd never seen before. Betsy had told me about how her parents had operatic, screaming fights when she was a kid, but this next generation seemed very polite. Even so, I felt tired and disoriented, worried that one of my sleek-looking in-laws would ask me what I did for a living. Of course no one did.

Except for mild irritation with my driving Betsy had displayed no emotion all day, and in the van after dinner I asked her why. She had done her grieving before now, she said. Her mother had been gone long ago, and now Betsy wanted to be the kind of mother Molly had been to her. What Molly's premature death showed her was how little time any of us have.

That night Betsy stayed up late talking with her brother and sister. In bed I rolled myself up in a blanket for shelter from the air-conditioning and read poetry that extolled the natural world in all its pullulating glory, birds and wilderness and the inexorability of plate tectonics. The poet's cosmic view seemed to point out all my trivial feelings of insecurity.

The birds and the continents were moving on — just like the boys, running headlong into a life of aunts and uncles and new experiences. I seemed to be the only one trapped in the past, unable to let it go. Like the future, the past was a dark place, but it was also a stable one: nothing changed there, no one demanded anything of me.

III

When we arrived back in Winnipeg I had to take the cats to the vet for their annual shots, buy a month's supply of table wine, and get the car stereo fixed. We'd replaced the factory one but the new radio made hissing noises whenever we listened to AM. I'd taken it back once already and the technician claimed nothing was wrong.

"Then why does it still hiss?" said Betsy. "They should fix this. We spent a lot of money there."

"Yeah but they have no obligation."

"You have to push a little. Call him back."

"They sell these things every day. They won't do anything."

"Why can't you assert yourself? Talk to the manager."

"I'm not calling him back. They already re-wired it once. So we listen to CDs now or FM."

Her eyebrows went up. Betsy listened almost exclusively to AM radio.

"I could go back there I guess."

"You guess?"

"I think it's pointless."

"Well which is it?"

"Don't yell at me. I don't do that to you."

"Not yelling doesn't make you any better, it just makes you more like your father."

"That's not fair!" I yelled. "There! I'm yelling! Is that what you want?" As I stomped off I saw the boys in the next room staring at me. They looked worried. They weren't the only ones.

—

I met Betsy in the spring of 1998. She came to the gym at R.B. Russell High School on a Wednesday night to scrimmage with my senior men's basketball team. She scored on me several times from the top of the key and my teammates trash-talked me. I became more aggressive on defence and bumped heads with her, but she kept scoring. Within a week I asked her out, intrigued by a woman who was both highly educated and athletic, and beautiful.

After we'd dated for two months, Betsy came for dinner at my apartment. I cooked dinner and also picked about a dozen pieces of music to play on my stereo for her, each record marked with a yellow Post-it note: Louis and Ella singing "The Nearness of You," Chet Baker's soft, sensual trumpet on "If I Should Lose You," Jimi Hendrix playing "Little Wing." We ate chicken curry — one of two or three meals I could cook — and I told the story of each piece: where I first heard the music, bought the record, details of the artist's life.

After dinner we held hands on the floor in front of the stereo. Betsy's hands were dry and strong. I imagined putting them on my face and crying. But I couldn't express my feelings, even to Betsy, so openly. What I could do was play songs eloquent with emotion, songs that said all the things I couldn't say.

I had not planned a seduction. But Betsy stayed with me that night. I felt grateful and stunned.

The next morning Betsy got up early and went to her office. I watched a videotape of *Let's Get Lost*, the Chet Baker documentary. Baker's sadness, his sunken face, his self-destruction, they all got to me that morning. Betsy called and I cried. I was in love with her, vulnerable in a way I didn't remember being since before adolescence.

For months afterward, every time we made love I made a small x in my daybook, as if living in the present was more than I deserved.

In the fall, after four blissful months of dating, Betsy asked me if I wanted to have children with her. She did not want to get more deeply involved with me if our relationship couldn't include children. The topic did not surprise me. I knew she loved kids. She talked a lot about her experience coaching them on basketball teams, her ideas about child-rearing. And, like Captain Hook, I knew about ticking clocks. Gazing at her intense, narrow face I hesitated. I had a sudden vision of my father, diving off a twenty-foot cliff into apparently shark-infested waters when we lived in Jamaica.

I said yes, I'd love to have children. As long as I had time to write. Betsy assured me I would. I loved and trusted her, and above all, didn't want to lose her. But seven years and two kids change many things. We no longer fell into each other's arms when the lights went out — more often than not she fell asleep, while I brooded over our lost romantic past. If I complained about our sex life she said she needed me to *engage* with the boys and our family life. I found myself thinking longingly of all those xs in my daybook.

My parents finally came to visit in July. I was walking home with the boys from the corner grocery when I saw Mom and Dad waving from their van. Peter and Bohdan jumped into the vehicle through the big middle door, opening it themselves and trapping my parents in their seats with enthusiastic hugs. After my father disentangled himself he hugged me, an unusual gesture.

During the past year Mom had started obsessing over small details. She'd only drink one particular brand of bottled water that I hadn't been able to find in Winnipeg, and had brought only a limited supply. With a sudden abandonment of the topic, she said she wanted to make borscht for us and insisted our bone-in beef ribs, which she hadn't even seen, weren't good enough. One crisis at a time, I thought.

I drew Mom a little map to the grocery store around the corner, a five-minute walk. Half an hour later she wasn't back, so Dad and I went looking. We found her half a block away at the street corner, holding the sirloin beef strips in a bag, uncertain which way to go, staring at the traffic on Maryland Street.

Over the two days they stayed with us, I noticed Dad working a lot in the kitchen. He kneaded the dough for the white buns Mom always made with borscht. Then he helped her shape the dough so each bun had a little knob on top, the way she baked them when I was a boy. I'd never seen my dad cook anything before; the most he did in the kitchen was to dry the dishes that Mom washed. But instead of asking Dad about his new kitchen duties or Mom's memory problems, I talked to him about where to park their van, how to place fans so Mom wouldn't be too hot at night, what to eat for breakfast that wouldn't upset her stomach.

The boys took to my parents right away. Bohdan stroked Dad's bald head while sitting in his lap. Peter chattered so fast none of us could understand him. During our final dinner, while we ate the last of the borscht, a work crew insulated the back wall of our kitchen. The injection tool made a sound like an amplified rubber cup hitting a board. Bohdan turned pale. Then he got up from the table, which was against the rules.

"You need to sit down, Bohdan," said Betsy.

"Nee likey." He pointed to the kitchen, where the sounds got louder.

"What's he saying?" asked my mom. Neither of my parents spoke a word of Ukrainian.

"Took, took, took," said Bohdan, "No likey." He covered his ears.

"He hates loud noises," I said. "Don't worry, Bohdan. They're working on our house to make it better." I put him back on his booster seat. He was still short for his age and his English was more limited than Peter's.

"Bohdan is scared," said Peter, recognizing the problem.

"He and Bohdan haven't had a single fight since they got here," I said to my folks. I'd told them very little about our difficulties with the kids. "They are very good brothers."

"They love borscht," said Mom.

"Smetana?" asked Bohdan, and I passed him the sour cream that he ladled into his soup in glogs the size of his fist. He didn't care about the *took took* sounds now. Peter used both hands to shake Tabasco sauce into his bowl. The smell of dill and hot butter and baking rolled over us.

———

After my parents left, I took out Dad's autobiography that he'd written in 1999 and read it again, looking for the connection that always seemed to elude us when we were together. The document consisted of nine single-spaced pages with the title "A Personal History: My Search for Freedom." He had prepared it to present as a sermon in church. His style was abstract — "I had within me the ability to decide to be free" — and resolutely distant. He told crucial stories in summary, never lingered on sensual detail, and never revealed his feelings about even the trivial events. The traumatic ones he intellectualized. Like father, like son.

He described his experience of the Soviet army's invasion in 1945, when he was eight years old, like this:

> *My most vivid memory of the Russian Army was not the sight of soldiers raping women, which I did not understand, but the sight of soldiers throwing hand grenades into our beautiful lake and killing its innocent fish. THAT I DID understand!*

Dad told me this story when I was in my twenties. When I asked who these women were, he said they were strangers. I'd written a poem then about his story, trying to make something out of the splinter of narrative:

Soldiers

*They marched wobbling into our yard, drunk
as the fish in the pool. They threw grenades*

*into the water, lily-pads exploding in soft white pieces,
frog heads jumping on the grass.*

*That afternoon they lay on top of our neighbour's wife
while she screamed more and more quietly.*

In the last couplet I'd accidentally hit on a historical truth. The neighbour's wife *was* raped, according to Lil. But then, so were most of the women and girls.

—

One of the things I had hoped for when I first read Dad's autobiography was some explanation for why he'd trotted our family around the globe so relentlessly, and what role, if any, my mother played in those decisions. Mom told me that after finishing his doctorate, my dad had declined a tenure-track university position. Before she began losing her memory, she often wished for the pension that would have gone with that job.

When I asked him why, he said his religious convictions had led him to work for the American Bible Society in Africa. But his autobiography revealed that he had developed other, less orthodox ideas about God. I couldn't believe that God told him to reject job security, or to jump off cliffs.

I also wondered why, in the late 1960s, we had not returned to Africa. As a kid I'd wanted to stay in a hot country, a place with no winter: we would have gone to Congo, a hotter place than I understood at six years old. Occasionally he did choose the safer path. His autobiography explained our sudden removal from Africa in the summer of 1968 this way:

> . . . *we came to a very difficult decision, which was not to return to Africa where we had all suffered from either malaria, intestinal parasites, or stomach ulcers. I began to feel very uncertain about my hopes for a career in the field of linguistics, and worse still, I had developed a serious problem in my failure to communicate adequately with my wife.*

In her diary from the same period, Mom wrote: "Eric told me he has decided NOT to go back to Africa." She made no reference to Dad's "failure to communicate adequately," nor to her endless complaints about living in Africa, or her impassioned prayers for God to deliver her from tropical illness. But later she often alluded darkly to that year as a *troubled time* in their marriage.

My father landed back in Winnipeg assembling cabinets at A.A. DeFehr Furniture for $1.60 an hour, ten hours a day, five days a week. We lived in a tiny apartment in North Kildonan and he gave violin lessons for extra money. My mother had escaped Africa but she was still miserable, and communicated that misery by slamming doors and banging pots in the kitchen. My father's diary ended on October 2, 1968.

Now I wondered if I was as remote a husband as my dad, but married to a woman who fought back and cursed instead of just praying for deliverance.

—

In the last week of August we went to a lake in eastern Saskatchewan to visit some friends of Betsy's. They were home on holiday from a CIDA assignment in Africa. We told Peter and Bohdan how nice and cool it would be swimming in the lake. The weather had been scorching hot for a month.

The man-made lake was invisible from even a mile away on the unchanging Saskatchewan plain. Close up it looked like a swamp where several giants had died, leaving only their pubic hair behind: the water was so full of algae blooms that no one ever went in. Betsy's friends Jim and Lenore had a family cottage here and a motorboat. With his beard and flip-flops, Jim reminded me of what my dad looked like when we lived in Jamaica in the '70s. He pulled the kids through the algae-clogged lake on a big rubber tube behind the motorboat. Peter and Bohdan wore lifejackets and shrieked with delight as Jim pulled them in big circles through the dank, shallow water.

Betsy and I sat on shore watching the lake in separate deck chairs as if we were seniors in a Cialis commercial. After Jim came in on the boat he called Bohdan and Peter to him and they jumped on his lap. I was surprised how little they hesitated — they'd just met him an hour earlier. He roughhoused with them, yanking their hair and arms, turning them upside down, making them squeal with delighted laughter.

I felt jealous of Jim's ease with the boys, but also uncomfortable with the physical play; my dad never roughhoused with me, nor had I with Jeremy. Dad did play with me often, usually building sandcastles or Lego forts. An only child, Jeremy had played on his own.

At night the cottage felt like a steam room. Our bedding was damp in the first hour from humidity and sweat. The four of us slept on the floor and waves of mosquitoes attacked us like the Luftwaffe over England. There were so many they formed black clouds on the ceiling.

Just before school started I took Peter to the Health Sciences Centre in Winnipeg for a follow-up on his positive test for tuberculosis.

The boys and I drove to the hospital early so we'd have time to park. The clinic's large waiting room brimmed with kids and toys, and the boys were excited. While I read a magazine, they climbed on a miniature slide made for toddlers. Bohdan dove down the slide head first and got stuck while Peter pushed his feet from the top. They both whooped. A toddler tried to get on the slide, but she couldn't get them to move. I showed them some toys on the floor, but they were distracted by a riding car in the next room. Soon Bohdan pushed Peter in the car at high speed past the desk and into one of the examining rooms. I followed to impose a time-out, frustrated at having to be in a constant state of vigilance. Jeremy hadn't been like this; from a very young age he sat still when we had to wait, allowing me to read or gather my thoughts.

We were called into an examination room right after the time-out; it had been only ten minutes. The nurse who saw us first was patient with Peter's fidgeting and nervous chatter. She took him for a new lung x-ray; the tiny one they'd had on file in Ukraine never made it to Canada.

A few minutes later the doctor arrived with the new x-ray and Peter. Peter wanted to go into a long description of the x-ray machine, but I held his hand and asked him to let the doctor talk first. Bohdan sat on my lap shifting his position every few seconds.

The doctor said Peter had only gotten a three-month regimen of the powerful antibiotic isoniazid in Ukraine. I knew that positive skin tests weren't unusual — my father and his brother Helmut both had positive tests in 1948 when they came to Canada, although they did not have TB antibiotics then. Peter, however, had to go back on the drug, this time for the standard nine-month period. A public health nurse would visit our house every week to administer the pill.

———

The public health nurse who brought Peter's medication every Monday at noon was Rose, a blonde with a cheerful dimple in her chin. Peter had no trouble swallowing the two kinds of pills, even the capsules bigger than his thumb. He and Bohdan both enjoyed taking medicine of any kind. In the orphanage, visits by the doctor had been one of the few times they got sustained individual attention from an adult. Both of them hugged and kissed me and Betsy when we administered routine cold remedies or children's aspirin.

Peter became very attached to Rose. He would sit on her knee and describe his morning and his lunch, then happily dispatch the inch-long white pills, smiling with a look of rapture on his face. He would wait a few seconds to prove his mastery and then stick out his purple tongue, and then he'd wash the medicine down with a glass of milk.

IV

In September the boys started school, Bohdan in nursery and Peter in kindergarten. That year seems like a mostly-forgotten dream now, shimmering and in soft focus around the edges like a tacky studio photograph. The boys were affectionate, grateful, rarely angry, seldom whining. They ate astonishing amounts of food. Apart from the occasional rambunctious outburst, they were compliant.

I walked the boys to school in the morning and picked them up at noon. The walk took about ten minutes for a grownup alone and about half an hour with the boys. Since Bohdan was barely two feet tall and I was over six, I had to list over like a sinking ship to hold his hand. If I did not hold his hand he'd wander into people's yards, approach animals regardless of size or menace, investigate parked cars at close range, or suddenly dart across the street.

I held Peter's hand too, but as he was older I tried to control him by gently asking him to stay close. At some new sight, though, he would yank hard on my arm like a leashed dog who suddenly sniffs an exotic scent.

Holding the boys' hands I felt protective and proud, and I noticed new things about my neighbourhood: the orange tabby cat on Palmerston who did happy-rolls on the sidewalk, the crows who lived in one particular back alley squawking like academics at a conference, the young couple who cursed at each other every Tuesday at 11:50 am in a parked Saab from the 1980s.

—

Every day when we got home I prepared the same lunch: for the boys, two hot dogs cut in half-inch lengths and simmered in generic chicken noodle soup, and for myself, scrambled eggs and coffee. The boys drank milk and talked about what they'd seen on the walk. I tried to be more like Betsy, taking part in the conversation, but most of my energy went into crowd control, since food flew and limbs flailed around the table.

Three days a week at one o'clock the babysitter, Ruth, arrived in her ten-year-old white Cavalier. She was a matronly woman in late middle age, a widow with a hoarse voice who had done childcare for one of our neighbours. Ruth took the boys to movies and to McDonald's play structures, new activities for Peter and Bohdan. When she stayed home with them they played in the basement together, on the far side from the water heater, pushing toy trucks around and building Lego structures, while I worked upstairs.

Every few weeks Betsy would say, you need to play with the boys when they ask, and occasionally I did. But I lacked Ruth's patience; the boys' enthusiasm level included stamping on my hands, or sitting by accident on someone's else's toys, or shouting "Dad, Dad" at rock concert decibel levels to ensure my attention. Sometimes Peter even yelled "Mom" at me, as if indifferent to my exact identity. I loved their intensity but it was like the equatorial sun: only a few minutes of exposure and you had to withdraw. My father had withdrawn as well, to his study, to his violin, but Betsy said he'd had better reasons than I did: a past that shut him down in some crucial way, a career that went off the tracks, and now an ailing wife. She was right, but I was still angry to hear her say it.

On Saturday mornings I'd play basketball outside with some of my friends. The boys tagged along so Betsy had time to make meals for the week. One Saturday we drove to the north end for a game. I had a deal with Peter and Bohdan: they were to play quietly and not interrupt my game — unless one of them started bleeding; I would buy them each two dollars' worth of candy at 7-Eleven after one hour of basketball.

Back in the car to begin the sugar festival, Peter noticed an old Buick in the parking spot beside us, up on jacks with the tires missing.

"Why is that car there? Dad, why don't you move it?"

I looked at his face in the rear-view mirror. No sign of joking.

"How would I move the car?" I asked.

"Dad, leeft up," said Bohdan, fists clenched like a cartoon character and making a lifting motion.

"You guys know that car weighs a lot, right?" I'd spent the last decade striving to put five pounds of muscle weight on my angular frame, and I felt touched by their faith in me.

"Dad, you can do it!" Peter insisted.

"I'm not Superman. I'll just have to leave that car alone." They both looked stunned at my refusal to even try flexing my giant biceps.

For the past two months I'd been doing commercial writing as a contractor for a virtual advertising company. What made the company virtual was that it consisted entirely of a stylish young woman who told her clients that she was "100% cheaper" because she had no office. That discount included my hourly rate. The copy I wrote luridly described a miracle construction product for insulating walls. But most of my billable time was taken up by meeting with the client at a Boston Pizza in north Winnipeg, where I drank bottomless Sprite and peed every ten minutes or so. Once when the client, a large jocular man with red hair, said that I could probably go to Hawaii on all the work he would give the virtual agency, I made the mistake of saying that my real work was writing poetry and what I did for him was just an interruption. The stylish young woman from the virtual agency stopped calling me.

———

One night a week I took Jeremy out for fast food so we'd have some time on our own to talk about school, the band he'd joined, the music he listened to. Betsy had the idea; she worried that Jeremy might feel neglected. Jeremy was Sid Vicious-skinny and almost six feet tall now, with his hair long and duck-tailed around the edges. His band had recently renamed themselves the Fops. Before that they were Orange Pendek, which according to Jeremy meant nothing, and according to Google meant Malaysian bigfoot. I told him how Peter and Bohdan screamed on the plane when we landed in Winnipeg, and suggested they consider the name Screaming Ukrainians. He laughed, the first time in at least two years he'd laughed at anything I said. Then he invited me to his gig on Friday night.

Jeremy's gig was in the small gymnasium of a Chinese community centre downtown. The audience was me, Betsy, and two dozen teenagers who pretended they were somewhere else, maybe an airport in a foreign country. The lead guitar player for the Fops was husky and tall, with dark hair falling on his face and shaggy eyebrows, his mouth open in a slash while he flailed at a guitar and screeched off-key into a microphone. He had two amplifiers stacked up and the noise bounced painfully off the concrete floors and walls. Between songs he made cryptic remarks that Jeremy and the bass player laughed at.

The fact that Jeremy could play the drums, any instrument at all, delighted me, since he hadn't practised much in the four years I'd taken him to drum lessons, or the year of piano lessons before that. It had been an area of conflict between me and his mother — she hadn't wanted to be the parent who said YOU MUST PRACTISE. But neither did I, and since Jeremy lived mostly with her, that's where his drum kit stayed.

Jeremy's band played only original tunes, and I couldn't understand any of the words. Where my father had played lyrical, romantic music on the violin, reaching for a lost world, Jeremy's music sounded like a series of car bombs. Now Dad spoke to Jeremy on the phone, and said to me that I was too hard on my son; was that the message in the echoing industrial noise of the gym?

We stayed until the bitter end, and I clapped Jeremy on the shoulder by way of a compliment. In the crisp fall air walking back to the car, I remembered playing half-clever parodies of the blues at an art gallery twenty-some years ago with my own band. The music Jeremy played was not clever. But it spoke without words, in the deafening shimmer of his crash cymbal above the tangle of snare, guitar noise, and angry screams.

At our weekly dinners, Jeremy never really told me what was on his mind. Of course, there were lots of things I'd never told him: that I'd hated high school as much as he had, or that I felt sorry for ignoring him so much when he was a kid, or how it felt when he held my finger in his baby incubator, born six weeks premature, his face indented and yellow. I never told him that fatherhood had not been in my plans when he came along. These were things I couldn't talk about, although I tried to in my poems, the same way my father had with his violin, and Jeremy did with his band.

—

One afternoon I was in my study while the boys played downstairs with Ruth. Shouting broke out and Bohdan ran up from the basement.

"My tooth!"

I gazed into his mouth. He'd lost a molar on the right side.

"Where is it?" I asked. I had a little plastic tooth container from the dollar store with a carrying string at the ready.

"I don't know," said Bohdan, with his elegant old world shrug, as if I'd just asked him for an explanation of general relativity.

"OK, we'll call Mom, and then we'll find it," I said, knowing Betsy would want to share the moment. It was a brief call; Bohdan still tended to nod on the telephone without speaking.

Downstairs, Bohdan said that the tooth was in the bathroom but he didn't remember where. Ruth confirmed that when the extraction took place he'd been in the bathroom with the door closed, at least she thought so. I began the search under Bohdan's direction while she kept playing with Peter. Bohdan pointed under the clawfoot bathtub, so I got down on my hands and knees on the hard floor and peered under the tub. Then I got a flashlight: nothing but dust bunnies and abandoned toys.

Then Bohdan pointed under the sink. The pipe went straight into the wall and the drain into the floor. I went on all fours again, minutely searching every square centimetre of the rock and pinewood floor, a very uneven surface. Nothing. I put the plastic tooth container around Bohdan's neck and he kept inspecting the floor.

Something like ten minutes had elapsed from the start of the search when Bohdan began elaborate head-scratching gestures. He pointed behind the toilet, in the corner where the toilet brush sat undisturbed amid archaeological spider remains. My optimism faded.

I took Bohdan by the shoulders and put my face close to his. "Do you really remember where you put the tooth?" His expression was serious and he went to the sink.

"I wash my hands," he said, narrating a sequence. "I go here." He walked to the bathtub. "Oh, I go out here." He left the bathroom into the play area, where a huge mess of toys sprawled on the dingy indoor-outdoor carpet.

Again I bent down to his head level and asked him to tell me what he remembered. He smiled with the same angelic look the baby Jesus has in religious paintings of the Italian renaissance. I was starting not to trust this expression. After a few more minutes of futile searching, I gave up and called Betsy again. We agreed that even though it was upsetting not to have his first baby tooth, we'd just have to live with it. And the tooth fairy could come anyway.

Just as I got off the phone, Bohdan came pounding up the stairs. "I find eet!" He was holding a large, yellowed molar.

"Where did you find it?" I asked.

"I show," he said, grabbing my hand. He took me to the toy shelf in the basement and pointed triumphantly eastward, at the wall.

"Did you know all along it was here?" He responded with his shit-eating grin again, like Bertie Wooster coming out of the Drones Club with someone else's umbrella, and nodded slowly.

"And you just let me keep looking and looking?"

Bohdan widened his eyes and bobbed his head just once. He smiled and my mouth also relaxed into a grin. I put the tooth in its plastic holder, told him we'd put it in his special box. I called Betsy to give her the good news. She was delighted and made me promise not to tell Bohdan about the tooth fairy until she got home.

—

We held off taking the boys to the dentist for several months because we wanted them to have enough English to understand what would happen. We'd seen no toothbrushes in either of their orphanages, and in that absence we didn't worry much for several reasons: Peter had no experience with brushing, he had a voracious appetite, and we believed he had a mouth full of fillings, since many of his teeth were a gunmetal grey colour.

When we did get to the dentist, Betsy and I stood beside the big white chair while Peter flipped switches and grabbed equipment. He refused to be still. The dentist wanted x-rays, so the assistant had Peter bite down on a piece of rubber. Peter couldn't keep his mouth closed. No x-ray was possible.

The dentist said that Peter's grey teeth, and the dark splotches on the biting surface of his molars, were actually abscesses. Most of Peter's baby teeth were rotten, he couldn't say exactly how many. Our dentist, possibly the gentlest and kindest person in the profession, referred us to a specialist in children's dentistry "who uses restraints when necessary."

A few weeks passed before we could see the specialist. At night Betsy and I talked with fear about *restraints when necessary*, and with guilt for all the months we didn't know Peter was in such pain.

When I shook the specialist's hand he had the vigour and bonhomie common among athletes and those who work with pliers and drills in people's mouths. Peter chatted away unworried, making the chair go up and down and gawking at the construction crane out the window.

The dentist encouraged Betsy and me to leave the room, and soon had an x-ray of Peter's mouth. All twenty-four of Peter's teeth had decay, but the eight molars were particularly bad, needing root canals and caps. The dentist said Peter likely had a high level of pain tolerance, because all his eating must have been hurting him. He didn't think anyone had ever brushed Peter's teeth before we adopted him.

He recommended doing the work with Peter under general anesthetic, at the hospital. The alternative was six or seven excruciating visits to his office, with restraints in use every time.

———

The day of the surgery Bohdan and Peter played on the floor in the hospital waiting room with toys intended for infants. This embarrassed me even though I understood why kids who'd missed part of their childhood would do that.

The dentist was behind schedule. We read stories to the boys and they sprawled on our laps. An extra hour passed and it was mid-afternoon. Finally the dentist appeared, wearing scrubs but with that air of sportiness about him. He shook my hand, nodded at Betsy, and chatted with Peter. Like me, Peter gabbed even more than usual when nervous. Betsy, Bohdan, and I gave Peter hugs. Bohdan pinched him on the bum. Then Peter climbed on a gurney.

I stared at the Assiniboine River, muddy and swollen still, no sign of the winter ice that would cover it in the coming months with a thick layer like a massive, multilayered blanket. Behind me Bohdan jumped on Betsy's lap. Every few minutes he asked for his brother. They were so attached to each other that Bohdan disliked being separated from him even at school.

Then Peter came wheeled out to us on a hospital bed, beginning to awaken. His face was puffed up purple with swelling, like a tabloid celebrity after plastic surgery. He tried sitting up and the nurse gently eased him down again. He smiled when I held his hand.

The nurse handed Peter a Beanie Baby. A tag pinned to its chest said *Courage Dog*. He held the plush cotton to his face.

"He hasn't complained about anything," said the nurse. Betsy and I both held his hands, and Bohdan stood as close as possible, staring fearfully at his brother's face. Within half an hour of arriving home Peter was already eating crackers. When we expressed some concern, he said this was the first time he'd been able to chew food without his teeth hurting.

▄

When I was four I had my tonsils out. I woke up on a gurney high off the floor in the hallway of the Baptist Hospital in Ogbomosho, Nigeria. My throat burned, head thick with sleep. My stomach felt wrenched inside-out. I looked down and around. No one. I didn't see my parents or any nurses. The big, bright red tiles got closer. I was falling. Then my father appeared, holding my hand, singing to me, the tune he played on his violin. I wasn't scared anymore. It hurt too much to talk.

I fell back into sleep. When I woke again Dad was still there, and he'd made a plasticine animal for me to play with when he'd gone. When he left I cried.

Dad said in his diary that I only shed tears on the operating table "till the ether took over."

▄

Bohdan turned four in Canada. It was the first time anyone had ever celebrated his birthday, as far as we knew. We invited more than twenty people, including Jeremy, the boys' godparents and their dog, several neighbours, the boys' Ukrainian-speaking babysitter and her whole family, and several of their Ukrainian-Canadian friends. Everyone brought a present. Jeremy arrived late with a large, beautifully wrapped package. Bohdan's eyes kept getting more dilated and he could not sit still. Peter helped carry the Safeway Spider-Man cake into the dining room, where we sang happy birthday loudly in the dark and watched Bohdan blow out his four candles. Just as the lights came back on my father phoned to wish him a happy birthday. My mother could not remember Bohdan's name.

There weren't enough chairs in the living room so half of us stood while we watched Bohdan open his presents. The grownups drank wine, the kids had soft drinks. The dog blundered around the living room, stepping on plates and barking. A guest dropped her wine glass on the hardwood floor and Betsy fetched the broom to sweep up the shards while I held the dog's collar. Meanwhile Bohdan tore the wrapping off one gift after another. One was a fire engine and we never did find the battery holder after that night. If Peter was jealous, we couldn't tell. Both boys radiated joy and good health.

—

A week later it was Halloween, something Peter and Bohdan had never experienced. Betsy had fun finding furry zip-up costumes for them at the local Salvation Army store, a dog outfit for Peter and a mouse costume for Bohdan. The boys wanted to wear the costumes all the time, and we let them bark and squeak as much as they liked. Betsy trained them to say trick or treat loudly while holding their pillowslips open wide to receive candy. We all laughed at the outrageous idea that total strangers would give them treats.

I did not go trick or treating in my childhood, nor did I ever wear a costume. For Mennonites — even my globe-trotting, liberal parents — the whole business of Halloween carried a whiff of the pagan. After Betsy zipped the boys tightly into their costumes and headed down the block, I enjoyed handing out candies at our door with the same cheerful *Happy Halloween* greeting for every tiny princess and toddling monster.

At home the boys dumped their pillowcases out on the living room rug. Betsy told me that Peter had stared open-mouthed as one of our neighbours poured candy into his pillowslip, and Bohdan was equally shocked but quicker to recover. They never noticed the cold. Bohdan displayed the effects of a sugar high before he unwrapped a single thing, running around the room and laughing crazily. We limited them to about half a dozen pieces each that night. Then we brushed their teeth and put them to bed. I kissed their heads and pinched their cheeks, and noticed they had that fresh-hay-and-milk smell that little boys do.

▬

Peter's tuberculosis treatment ended that spring when he was six. He was anxious when the final dose of the final week arrived. Betsy and I knew he would miss seeing the nurses. We'd bought a cake and planned to have a little ceremony. Rose came on that last day, a bit breathless at the door, knowing Peter would want to be fussed over. As Peter quickly dispatched the last of the medication, Bohdan watched me light candles on the cake in the kitchen. There were nine candles, one for each month he'd taken the pills. Bohdan and I marched the cake into the dining room, where Peter blew out the candles and I cut a piece for each of us. When it was time for Rose to go, Peter accompanied her to the door. He gave her a long hug and told her that she smelled nice. Tears streamed down his face as she left. He looked like a child at a parent's funeral.

—

In spring 2006 we celebrated adoption day at the end of March. We told the boys stories of what they were like when we met them. Bohdan now referred to himself in Ukraine as a baby, as if that phase of his life were far away. Peter couldn't remember any Ukrainian words although he'd gone to Ukrainian school every Saturday for six months. He wanted to be a Canadian, he said. He wanted the future right away. When Betsy brought out the cake Bohdan celebrated the first anniversary of his adoption by plunging his fingers into the moist layers, eyes protruding with joy. At bedtime Betsy and I took turns hugging Bohdan and Peter tightly, over and over at their insistence.

—

That night Betsy and I lay in bed talking about Peter's first year in Canada. Peter seemed so content — he was almost a perfectly behaved child. Sometimes the boys had poor impulse control, Betsy said, but that was only natural after being so under-stimulated in the orphanage, and malnourished and neglected before that.

"And now everyone tells us how cute they are and how much they look like us," I said. Betsy fell asleep tucked in close to me.

Even though I worked mostly for free, I was a full-time writer, and even though my wife swore at me sometimes I knew she loved me. Here we were after five years of marriage with a beautiful family, and we hadn't even changed a diaper. This had to be good fortune.

V

Things started to go wrong for Peter in grade one. He had speech therapy in school because he could not enunciate certain sounds and because he talked so fast.

When excited he'd leave out parts of words, and even though he learned English with amazing speed, he was hard to understand. My father still had trouble making out what he said on the telephone.

Peter also began asking us why his mother did not keep him and Bohdan. At first we said that his mother just wanted what was best for them. But why, he insisted? Why could she not be their mother? He was relentless. We fended off his questions as best we could, thinking the whole story would be too much for him, but pretty certain he wouldn't give up.

▬

We got reports from school that Peter was pulling and eating half-consumed food out of the garbage at recess. But we'd heard that kids with an orphanage background often went through the trash or hoarded food. Peter complained about how he couldn't make friends and how lonely he was at recess. This wasn't surprising either for someone in a new culture, a new family, and a new language. At home both boys slept badly and after waking up to loud noises in the middle of the night, we insisted that neither one leave his bed until morning. Peter would wake up at 5:00 am and rummage through his toys in the bedroom until we removed them.

▬

In the second half of the year we got a call from school. A teacher had found Peter running gleefully by himself up on the third floor, where only older kids were allowed. Peter said that when he went for speech therapy, he'd discovered the elevator in the middle of the school. He took joy rides when he left the classroom for bathroom breaks and recesses.

The elevator rides seemed innocuous to me, like Babar cavorting in the department store. Babar had been an orphan too, and he recovered beautifully from that trauma, showing how civilized he was by wearing spats and suits. We talked to Peter and his teacher to make sure he stopped wandering the halls. He just needed more supervision.

But there were issues in the classroom too. Peter got up from his desk at random and wandered around the room dozens of times every hour, helping himself to other kids' books, and distracting the class. When we talked to him about his behaviour, he knit his substantial brows and looked away from us.

Then near the end of the school year, when Betsy was doing laundry, she found candy and cookie wrappers in Peter's clothes. They weren't things we had given him. He claimed that he'd picked them up in the schoolyard. His teacher said that kids were missing desserts from their lunch kits. It had been going on for a while.

When we confronted Peter a second time about the desserts he yelled and cried and denied stealing anything, this time looking straight at us with steely grey eyes. We asked the same questions over and over in different ways like professional interrogators and I felt guilty about our insistence.

Peter finally admitted to stealing the sweets. He did not seem remorseful, only upset that he'd been caught.

Betsy went to a make-it-right meeting at the school with Peter, the little girl who was one of his victims, and the principal.

The principal asked Peter to apologize for stealing the girl's cookies.

Peter turned red and hesitated. Then he said, in an emotionless voice, "Sorry I took your cookies."

"Can you tell Peter what you told me?" the principal asked the girl.

The girl was crying, but she spoke. "We don't have much money. I asked Mom for the cookies at the grocery store. When she bought them, then she had no money for bread for her sandwiches."

Betsy told me Peter had an aggrieved expression on his face while the girl spoke directly to him, as if he were the person who had been wronged. Betsy felt frightened. We'd heard about those kids adopted from Romania, that many of them had become criminals because of childhood neglect in their terrible orphanages. Later that week, after talking with Betsy, I made an appointment for us to see a psychologist we'd heard about who had many years' experience working with adopted kids.

—

The psychologist was booked for months ahead and we only saw her near the end of August 2007, before Peter started grade two. She ushered the boys into a playroom so we adults could speak privately. Her office smelled like Pine-Sol. She had the manner of an emergency room physician who has seen everything and yet remains alert, always asking questions.

What was the boys' history? How had they gotten to the orphanage? We told her the sketchy story we'd received, that their birth mother had abandoned them with a boyfriend, who then brought them to a hospital, from where they were sent to the orphanage. The mother lost her parental rights when she failed to appear in court. During Peter's three years with her, there was drinking and fighting in the home. She was homeless now, no one knew for sure if she was alive. The father was probably dead.

Did Peter overeat or hoard food? Well, we had noticed him hoarding the food he'd stolen in the last few months. And he'd probably gained weight from those extra stolen sweets. Now that we thought of it, he did seem obsessed with food: when we went out to eat he analyzed each dish with the enthusiasm of a restaurant critic.

Was he overly familiar with strangers, touching them indiscriminately? Yes. At first we hardly noticed, but he carried on charm campaigns with new teachers and people whose names he didn't even know.

Did he dismiss comforting gestures or refuse to ask for help? Yes. He tried to do everything for himself and resisted letting us touch him when he got hurt.

Did he vomit on purpose? Yes, recently, when he disliked our parenting decisions. Bohdan did it sometimes too.

Was he accident-prone? Definitely. His knees were bloody every week from constant falls and collisions.

Did he engage in nonsense chatter, incessant talk? Yes, he did. He frequently called me Mom, chanting "Mom, Mom, Mom," even though I corrected him and he already had my attention. Then he talked rapidly until he got multiple requests to stop.

Were there sleep issues? Did he have insomnia? Yes, he was starting to wake up at night and in the morning he'd have dark shadows under his eyes.

Did he have trouble making eye contact with us? Yes. Almost all the time, except when he lied.

Did he lie about perfectly obvious things? Yes, he did. Again we had noticed it only recently, although the first instance I could remember was when he denied playing with the water heater. Sometimes you could catch him in the act and he would deny it anyway.

She asked similar questions about Bohdan, but we had little trouble with Bohdan beyond his over-familiarity with strangers and fake vomiting. After the questions, she called Peter and Bohdan in and spoke while we stayed quiet. The boys went back to the playroom.

She told us that Peter had something called attachment disorder. She said it was common with kids who were adopted or in foster homes, and who'd experienced severe neglect or child abuse. Such kids often had a honeymoon period with their new families, when they acted independent and highly capable. Our honeymoon was over.

The problem, she said, was that Peter had learned early on that the adults in his life were not reliable. It affected his development of self-control and self-regulation. For most kids this development happens as if they are building a network of tracks, like a railway, that connects them to their parents and other important adults in their lives. You can't move the tracks easily once they're laid down, which doesn't matter if they're going in the right direction. But Peter's tracks, she said, didn't go anywhere, because he could not rely on the adults around him in his early childhood. There was no station at the other end for Peter, and the only cargo delivered was shame and fear at his helplessness. He felt lonely and terrified.

I thought of that Dylan lyric about when your train gets lost. Poor Peter, building tracks in his brain that went off into the abandoned, empty station of the past. He could trust only himself to make the trains run on time, though he had no scheduling authority. So he took charge of everything he could, including food shipments. He also needed to be fearfully alert at night in case something awful happened, some terrible derailment that would mean additional pain and suffering.

We wanted to know if Bohdan was affected too. The psychologist did not think so, since he was only three when we adopted him. Peter's problem was not just that he remembered too much of his life before adoption at age five, but that the tracks and switches in his mind had settled into survivalist programming.

Could Peter recover? Well, there was no cure. Your own history never disappears. But he could learn to cope with his past. It would be hard.

———

After the diagnosis, with Peter almost seven, we changed our approach. Betsy read books and blogs about adoption, and we both tried to implement the psychologist's suggestions. If Peter got upset or was caught doing something wrong, we insisted that he stay in the same room with us after we gave him a consequence so he could rely on us instead of developing a sullen independence alone in his room. We wanted him to love himself as much as we loved him.

During her reading of adoption blogs, Betsy learned that many adoptive parents of kids from Ukraine hired investigators to search out more information about their children's birth families. These investigators usually were translators like Oleg, who spoke English and Ukrainian, and understood how to navigate their country's dysfunctional government bureaucracy.

In December we agreed that we wanted to know more about the boys' background than the bare-bones story we'd been given so that, at the right time, we could share the information with Peter and Bohdan. Betsy made email contact with a Ukrainian investigator named Olga. We transferred a few hundred dollars by Western Union, and Olga travelled from her home in Kyiv to the west of Ukraine. She located the boys' maternal aunt and sent us a detailed report together with digital pictures attached to her email. But after reading it, we thought it was too soon to share the report with the boys.

—

Then early in 2008 Peter got caught stealing lunch desserts in school again. Because the psychologist connected Peter's stealing and food hoarding with his feelings of deprivation, and especially with the desire to know about his birth mother, we decided it was time to talk to him about her, however hard it would be for all of us. This time Betsy and I talked privately about what we'd reveal to him. It would not be everything, not yet.

Betsy sat beside Peter on our living room couch and said, "We understand that you have difficult feelings to deal with." I stood in the doorway to the hall and watched. He wanted to run out of the room and Betsy held him. Peter's body went rigid with tension and he tried punching her. "We're your parents, and we'll always make sure you have enough to eat," she said. He struggled to get out of her arms, kicking and spitting. Then he relaxed into her body and cried.

"You need to feel your feelings, Peter, and the desserts won't help you with that," said Betsy. "Have you been thinking about your mother again?"

Peter nodded. I loved his curving lashes, how they slowed the large tears that rolled down his cheeks, and I felt something break open inside me.

"Your mother left you for her own reasons," said Betsy, looking him in the eyes and holding his head with her hands. "She was really poor, and she drank too much alcohol. It did not mean she didn't love you. There is nothing wrong with you. Nothing."

He rubbed his big hands through his eyes and cleared his throat. "I don't know how she could have left me and Bohdan," he said, "even if she was poor and drank too much alcohol." I didn't know either and my guesses held no more comfort than his.

Betsy asked him if he felt angry at his mom. "I could never be angry at her," Peter said, shaking with sobs again. Bohdan stood in the doorway with me now and I reached down to hold his hand. He looked pale and scared. I was scared too. When Peter went into one of his rages, it was easy to imagine him at the age of sixteen, the most volatile and vulnerable member of a criminal gang. I knew that he'd suffered, that he was frightened to death of abandonment; but I was frightened to death at the thought of being the father of a criminal. I loved Peter, but he scared me.

Ever since the boys were four and six I had been driving them to Edmonton for spring break to visit their grandparents and my sister's family. Betsy stayed home because she had to teach her classes at university, and it gave her a break from the men in her life. The trip also gave me and the boys a chance to bond. On the way to Edmonton we always stopped for the night in Saskatoon, at a hotel with a waterslide and free breakfast. I relaxed the rules and the boys got to play DS continuously in the car. We ate meals at fast food restaurants, I played Jimi Hendrix and Glenn Gould on the car stereo really loud, and we all had fun.

That spring of 2008, at the end of March, we went to Edmonton again, our third trip to see my family. The trip was a nightmare. Peter argued with me if I asked him to reduce the volume on his games, or he repeatedly jabbed his knee in the back of my seat, or he argued with his brother about whose turn it was with the most desirable DS game. In turn I barked at Peter, and several times reached into the back seat and wrenched his arm hard to make him stop hassling Bohdan. At the hotel in Saskatoon I drank an entire bottle of red wine after the boys went to bed, and that night Peter tossed and turned so violently I threatened to move him into the bathtub with his pillow and sheets.

My parents lived in a suite attached to my sister and brother-in-law's house. Dad had built an extension so he and Mom could have their own kitchen, appliances, and dining room, but the boys and I slept on my sister Criselda's side of the house, which was much bigger.

As we pulled onto the driveway, Criselda came out to greet us. She had the same hazel eyes as my aunt Lil. She hugged the boys and me extravagantly, and then we hauled our things inside. Her husband Bart offered me a beer, which I happily accepted, and her daughter Katya, my niece, showed the boys a new video game.

Later we had dinner with my parents in their suite. My dad now did all of the cooking and serving of food. At the table the boys were stir-crazy from confinement in the car all day.

"Are they usually this loud?" my mother asked me, as if Peter and Bohdan weren't there. Her hands shook and she ate only thin strips of soy cheese and drank insipidly weak tea. She complained about a vague stomach ailment and how tired she felt.

"How is Mom doing?" I asked Dad as we cleaned up the dishes.

"She's OK." He shrugged, worried that Mom would hear him. To see my mother sitting and watching television while Dad cooked and cleaned astonished me. From the living room she kept repeating a story about one of my cousins from three years ago. My mother used to be sharp-eyed and sharp-tongued, and the best source of family gossip. It was depressing and painful to see her, stooped over, with her beautiful long fingers clenched in her lap. She had lost her keen mind and with it, most of her words.

The boys and I spent the next day at the wave park in the West Edmonton Mall. They went down the biggest, highest slides allowed by the park rules, and I felt frightened; I don't like heights, and the boys lacked any healthy fear. We spent a solid, enjoyable couple of hours together in the wave pool, letting ourselves be tossed over the giant artificial waves in rubber tubes, Bohdan shrieking, Peter attracting extra attention from the patrols when he got too close to the edge. Satisfied they were well-occupied, I snuck off to the chairs at the side to read a novel. That evening my sister asked us to have our meals on their side of the house, so that Mom wouldn't be overwhelmed by the boys' volume and energy level. Dad did not come over much because he needed to stay with Mom, Criselda informed me; Mom panicked without him in the suite.

The second day of our stay, the boys ate breakfast with me in my sister's kitchen, and then I left them to play with Katya's toys while I went to see my parents in their suite.

Mom sat mutely on the couch. She handed me the TV remote because she no longer knew how to operate it. I turned on "Days of Our Lives" for her and found my dad in the kitchen. He washed up their breakfast dishes and I dried, and we talked about the weather and the Lakers for a few minutes, as always. He put the kettle on the stove and motioned me to the table and we sat down.

"How is Peter doing?"

"He's good, mostly."

"Does he remember anything from before you adopted him?" This question surprised me.

"Not much. His first conscious memory is when they drove him in an ambulance away from his brother, to the older kids' orphanage out in the country. He was four and about eight months." I hesitated, then said, "What is your first memory?"

"Ah, that would be from the war." He paused and his facial expression stiffened under his white, closely trimmed beard. My father has pure blue eyes, just like mine. "I saw people shot

so they fell into a ditch. Later I found out that they were Jews."
He remembered the bodies falling down into the ditch, he said,
the thud as they landed.

"How old were you?"

"Four or five." He swallowed.

The whistle on the kettle blew then and Dad took Mom her
cup of hot water together with an herbal tea bag on a saucer. I
could hear them murmuring over the soap opera theme music.

On our last full day in Edmonton, disappointed that the
boys had not seen much of their grandfather, I proposed that the
four of us go together to the nearby YMCA and swim. Dad loves
swimming, although he didn't get out much anymore because of
Mom's condition, and the boys enjoyed the water too.

We went after dinner for a family swim hour when the pool
was divided up into open areas and reserved lanes. All four of
us got in the water, Dad and I just treading water and watching the kids. Bohdan floated on his back in the shallow end
and played with a toy he could retrieve by diving to the bottom.
Peter strayed toward the lanes reserved for people swimming
laps. I called to him from the shallow end to come back and he
ignored me. He did a lazy backstroke at random angles into the
pool, and the second time he bumped into a grownup, I yelled at
him. Then I got out of the pool and told Peter to get out. When
he still refused, I got in and picked him up, carrying him to the
corner while he shouted. In my peripheral vision I could see Dad
staring at us.

"That's it, Peter, you're in time-out. You have to pay attention to other people in the pool." His face was set in a stubborn
rictus and he acted as if he could not hear me. Dad, Bohdan, and
I played in the water for ten minutes more, then I invited Peter
back into the pool. He refused, and did not speak on the way
home.

The boys and I slept in a room in the loft that contained many of their teenage cousin Katya's toys from her childhood, and I had to constantly check on them after they went to bed to be sure they weren't playing instead of sleeping. On our last night I was trying to have a glass of wine with Criselda but had to keep getting up because I could hear them getting out of bed, talking loudly, and knocking over pieces of furniture. Once I found them putting on Katya's dress-up costumes and jewellery. After finally getting them settled, I joined my parents in their suite to watch the late news, and came back to the room just after eleven.

I opened the door to find Peter's DS and toys scattered all over his bed and Peter scrambling to get under his covers. Bohdan was pretending to sleep but he was in the wrong position. I yanked the DS out of Peter's hands, grabbed the toys and threw them out from under his covers while he began screaming. I put my hands over his mouth and said *"Stop,* what's wrong with you?"

Bohdan sat bolt upright in his bed, not pretending to sleep anymore. "If you do that to my brother, I won't go to sleep either!"

"Christ, Bohdan. You're not asleep anyway."

I spent half an hour threatening, negotiating, cajoling them. In the end I said fine, do what you want, and fell onto my bed for a few hours of exhausted sleep.

In the morning we started late because we'd overslept. We said a hurried goodbye to my parents and sister, called Betsy to let her know we were on our way, and then I steeled myself for the long ride home.

—

Our hyper-athletic cat Alty became ill and died that summer; the anti-social Ranger had died the previous year. Alty ignored the boys, and Ranger ignored everyone, so Peter and Bohdan never really bonded with them and hardly noticed their absence.

In September Betsy and I decided to find some kittens for the boys. Peter and Bohdan became the proud owners of a sibling pair of orphans. They'd been rescued from a barn where they were the lone survivors of their mother's disappearance. Their littermates had starved to death. They were so young they had to be bottle-fed. As a result, they loved being held on their backs.

Peter named his male kitten January, because he'd dreamed of having a white cat, and even though January was a gorgeous grey tabby, Peter stuck with his original name. Bohdan called his female cat Gracie Flames, for the orange highlights on her brown and white calico coat. Probably because the cats were theirs, the boys were much more affectionate with them than they'd been with Ranger and Alty, playing with them, stroking them, talking to them. When the cats started going outside, Gracie liked to bolt across the street and wander around the neighbourhood. Peter was especially gentle with January, who stayed mostly on our porch.

▬

That fall, when Peter was eight and Bohdan seven, we decided that it was time for them to begin walking to school on their own. We gave the boys detailed instructions about their route and how we expected them to behave. They left for school at twenty minutes to nine, just early enough to get in for first bell. We let their teachers know so they'd notify us immediately if the boys were late.

For two weeks everything seemed fine. Their teachers reported no tardiness, and the boys were cheerful and on time after school — we allowed twenty minutes to get home as well.

Then came a call from the principal. They had been spotted by other parents who saw them wrestling each other in the street, pulling lumber out of backyards, smashing bottles on the sidewalk, and screaming obscenities into apartment block intercoms. After lengthy and separate interrogations we found out that Peter was the instigator of these follies, Bohdan the good soldier. We put Bohdan under strict orders to report to us when his brother did crazy stuff. But he was foolishly loyal and maybe we asked too much of him. In any case Betsy and I resumed our old routine, Betsy playing chaperone in the morning, and I in the afternoon.

—

The boys went to daycare for the after-school program from 3:30 until 5:00, so I could write and do freelance work for a full day. The truth was that I had trouble handling them with Betsy away from home until dinnertime.

On a Tuesday afternoon in December I walked into the daycare centre a few minutes early and saw the boys playing together. Bohdan came skipping toward the door but Peter pretended not to see me. Somebody called him and pointed at me in the doorway. Peter ambled over.

"Hi Peter. We need to hurry home and get supper started," I said.

"Mm," he said, not meeting my eyes.

I recognized this response; he was in trouble for something, God knew what. Peter's teacher marked his agenda every day to tell us if he'd stayed in his desk when he was supposed to, and if he was on time for the start of class. When he didn't get his teacher's initials, his consequence was that he ate oatmeal and a plain slice of bread for dinner. He hated oatmeal, preferring chef's salad and exotic cheese. I felt sorry for him, but we'd tried everything else: incentive systems, deductions from his allowance, confiscating toys, tearful lectures. None of it worked. And we didn't want to use corporal punishment at all.

At the daycare locker Peter deliberately collapsed on the floor in giggles. Then he ran around the corner and hid. My stomach knotted up the way it had when I was seventeen and drank half a mickey of lemon gin as an experiment in losing control.

Bohdan meanwhile had quietly put on his winter things. It was so cold that exposed skin froze in two minutes. I had to stand over Peter to make him get ready. He kept looking up at me mockingly. After about ten minutes the boys and I left the daycare centre.

"I'm going to run away," Peter said. And he ran across the street without checking for traffic. I chased him, also without checking. Bohdan stood on the sidewalk watching us.

"You have to walk with me." I grabbed Peter by the shoulder and shook him hard.

"No I don't." He laughed. This time he ran up a back alley and I chased him again. He threw himself down and I pulled him to his feet and dragged him back along the icy sidewalk, my now ungloved hands stinging with cold. Someone came past us with a dog. I smiled as if to say that everything was under control.

Peter was a solid kid, and my arms ached from trying to frog-march him. Bohdan pulled on me from behind, while Peter giggled and thrashed, breathing in the painfully cold air.

"Bohdan, you've got to stop. I'm not hurting Peter. Let's go." Our breath hung above us like a storm cloud.

Peter stared at me defiantly from under his brows and shouted, "You can't make me go with you!"

He let his legs go limp and stared at me insolently, as if daring me to hit him. Then he ripped his hat from his head.

"Stop that," I bellowed. "You'll get frostbite, you little shit!"

Instead of twenty minutes the walk home took over an hour. I marched Peter in the front door with me instead of sending him to the back and gave him a hard push when he walked into the house. He fell theatrically on the floor in the front hall, then scrambled back to his feet and made a dash for the door. Bohdan jumped out of his way.

Peter careened into the wall as he tried to escape out the front door. Bohdan watched from behind me. I blocked the door and wrestled Peter down again, pinning his legs under mine so he couldn't move. We both gasped for breath, gulping in the warm air from the ancient steam heat system.

Just then Betsy walked in the front door and had to step over me and Peter sprawled out in the hallway. Over Peter's howls of rage, I told her what happened. Betsy did not hesitate.

"Do you still want to run, Peter?"

"Yes!" he said, with tears irrigating his face.

"Let him up, Maurice."

Peter shuffled to his feet.

"If you run away, Peter, you cannot take any money or toys, you know. And you will be lonely without Bohdan but he is too small to run away. Do you still want to go?"

Peter emptied his pockets onto the hardwood floor.

"And you will need your hat and mitts," Betsy said, putting them on Peter as she spoke, even though he resisted. "It's very cold. Do you still want to run away?" Peter wrenched open the door and ran down the street toward Maryland Avenue. Bohdan and Betsy and I stared at one another uneasily.

Every five minutes Bohdan asked where his brother went. Peter would be back soon, Betsy reassured him. But after Peter was gone twenty minutes I took Betsy aside. She was pale and worried, and said, "He's got to come back soon."

"I'd better go find him," I said, and she nodded, then went to heat dinner for Bohdan.

I searched for over an hour and then came home to see if Peter had returned in my absence. Bohdan lay in bed, crying,

Betsy beside him holding his hand and talking to him in a low voice. I left again, the cold and the fear tightening their vise-grip on my body. I had horrible visions of him frozen to death or worse. Then at the end of Sherbrook I saw a familiar bright red parka stepping out of a pawnshop. Peter turned and saw me, and sprinted for the back alley.

I cornered him in the dead end of the alley by the garbage cans, tackled him, and dragged him home by the waist, screaming and kicking at me the entire way. At nine when we finally got home Bohdan still lay awake. He was terrified.

VI

We decided to make the rest of December as quiet as possible and crossed everything off our calendars that wasn't essential. Betsy began coming home from work early so both of us would be there to pick Peter and Bohdan up from daycare; there would be no more experiments with letting him run. I locked our side door and hid the key so the house would have only one exit. Peter needed fewer options.

The first day that Betsy and I arrived at the daycare together, Peter came out in the hall without looking at us and sat down on the floor. I asked him to stand up. He did, but also put my hand on his head while he rammed it against the wall. It looked like I was pushing his head and so I snatched my hand back. Other parents in the hallway glanced nervously at each other.

Throughout the month Peter kept threatening to run away again. Bohdan clung to his brother in the day and cried every night. None of us slept properly. The third or fourth time Peter threatened to run, Betsy screamed at him. This time, in tears, she told Peter he was being a terrorist to our family. Peter grinned, although when I asked he could not define the word. Betsy forced herself to calm down and explained that a terrorist was someone who gets what he wants by making threats and even blowing things up, while Bohdan shook his head and sat by himself. To ourselves we would say that Peter was a terrorist of love, for love, and it was love and steady attention that he needed — every night while we drank large glasses of wine and binge-watched *The Sopranos* on DVD. Seeing people defend family values with violence seemed logical and satisfying.

When we went upstairs for the night, Betsy still read, but now she erected a Berlin wall of pillows between us. She was in peri-menopause, she said, and couldn't sleep properly if I put my arm around her: it made her uncomfortably warm. We also had a fan stationed in the bedroom now, even in winter. I looked up "peri-menopause" on the web and what she said made perfect sense. But it didn't make me happy.

We had regular fights about my incompetence doing household chores and what Betsy said was my bad attitude. In the past I'd challenged her to give me examples as they occurred, claiming that my failures were an occasional, infrequent result of absentmindedness and deadline pressure in my work. But now she gave me daily bulletins: I failed to turn up the furnace on some unpredictable mornings; I put food-encrusted dishes back in the cupboard; I spilled crumbs all over the couch while eating lunch; I snarled at her if she asked me for the third time *when* I planned to take out the garbage. At the height of our worst argument she said she'd been pulling most of the weight in the marriage, and now with the kids, for over a decade, and I needed to decide: was I in or out? Her voice shook with anger but her eyes filled with tears. What was wrong with me?

On Christmas Eve I walked with Peter to the corner grocery on Westminster, holding his hand because I still didn't trust him, even though he seemed relaxed.

"Why is December so hard for you?" I asked, looking down at his hood.

"I remember things," he said. "I remember with my body."

—

On the second Friday in January Peter and Bohdan had no school. It was my turn to take a day off work. I gave Betsy a hug as she left for the bus.

"That's a board hug," she said. I dropped my arms.

Later in the day I told the boys I'd take them sledding. I made hot chocolate in the microwave and put it in thermoses. We hauled the various plastic and wooden sleds from the basement to the garage.

It was so cold that you couldn't smell anything; the world was frozen, antiseptic. "La, la, La La LA LA LA," sang Peter, loudly, while dragging a sled along the side of the car, scraping the paint. I grabbed his arm hard enough that he could feel it through his down parka.

"Peter, you can't do that, you're eight years old — and you'll wreck the car."

We picked up Bohdan's friend Thomas, then drove to the toboggan hill. Thomas and Bohdan wrestled in the back seat and I had to force myself to calmly ask them to stop instead of screaming at them. They kept wrestling in the back seat. Peter sulked in the front. I had no idea how to control all this boy energy. My hands shook on the wheel.

When I parked, Bohdan almost rolled into the street together with Thomas and I had to physically separate them. Their relationship consisted of death-grip wrestling and complete disregard for their surroundings. Bohdan complained about Thomas's roughhousing but had a fatal attraction to him.

The wind whipped past me on top of the hill, penetrating every seam in my parka. My feet felt like frozen pylons within a few minutes, and the sky had that beautiful blue clarity it gets when the temperature is decades below zero.

Peter's mood hung like a toxic cloud. I announced that everyone had to go down the hill twenty times for hot chocolate, an irrelevance for Bohdan and Thomas, who were already running up and down the hill, but I wanted Peter to exert some energy so he'd cheer up.

"I don't want hot chocolate," said Peter. He rolled his eyes in an amazing simulation of a teenager and plunked himself down in the snow.

"Peter, you have to go down the hill right now. Or else." I had no idea what *or else* meant, but at least he got up and dragged his sled to the top of the run in slow motion. Then he proceeded down the hill in a lazy zigzag designed to annoy me. How long would I have to watch this performance?

As I sat on the hill and counted Peter's achingly slow ascents and descents, I got colder and colder and almost gave in at eighteen. He slouched up for his hot chocolate, then spilt half of it on my parka.

"Jesus Christ," I snapped, wiping off my coat with an already-grimy tissue. "You did that on purpose!"

"Sorry," Peter said with a grin of utter insincerity. Bohdan and Thomas grabbed each other near the top of the hill, on the iciest part.

"Get away from there!" I shouted. "It's dangerous!" They fell and rolled down the hill sideways, laughing, ignoring me.

When we got home after dropping off Thomas, I told the boys to change out of their snowpants and parkas. The phone rang just as I unzipped my newly-stained parka. Betsy. She was having a great day, productive, working with a colleague on a paper. How were we? Not so great, although I didn't say that. Peter walked into the living room still in his boots, dragging a sled behind him and yelling at Bohdan. I tossed away the phone and wrenched him off his feet, carrying him and the plastic sled to the basement landing, and plunked him down hard. It felt good. The sled fell down the stairs in a big clatter.

"You do that again and I'll sit on your head, do you understand?" I was shaking him and his face was white. He yanked on my parka and it tore from collar to zipper with a sharp rip. Bohdan jumped on my back to stop me from attacking his brother. I turned, put Bohdan down on the floor and he ran off. Then I told Peter, who was boo-hooing, to shut up and stay seated on the landing. I walked back to the phone in the living room.

"You still there?" I said, loudly. Yes she was.

"I can't goddamn well do this." My voice shook and I had to pause. "I'm afraid I'm going to hurt Peter. He just won't listen."

"Maurice, can you control yourself?" I was hyperventilating on the phone like an obscene caller. "Look. I'm coming home."

"Oh God, you must be kidding. You've got work to do. That's the whole point of me having them today."

"Can you control yourself?" she asked again.

"Yeah, yes. Yes I will."

Peter and I both had a time-out, lying on our beds staring at the ceiling for half an hour. I calmed down. Betsy stayed at work. I hugged Peter and Bohdan and promised them not to lose my temper again. Their faces were limp and shell-shocked but I suppressed my rage enough to get through the afternoon up to Betsy's return. I had never seen my own father lose his temper, and didn't understand where my quick-trigger fury came from.

On the weekend Betsy walked into the kitchen waving a snow shovel. "I really need you to put away the shovels properly."

"Do we have to talk about that now? You know I'm going out." I often went to book launches or readings, leaving Betsy to put the boys to bed.

"We've talked about this before. When you leave the shovels and rakes leaning all over the tool room, I have to stack them up before getting to the one I need. I feel like you don't care about me, since you know I do most of the shovelling."

"Christ, they're just tools. Why are you ascribing symbolic meaning to the arrangement of shovels and rakes?" I said in my best Christopher Hitchens mode. "You're making a category error. In a poem it would make sense, because in a poem everything is meaningful. In real life not so much."

"What if your wife disagrees?"

"Then with all due respect to my wife, she's just wrong. Some things are trivial and meaningless."

"So my feelings are trivial and meaningless. There's your tactic one — dismiss my concerns. Why don't you ever listen to me?"

"Oh come on, Betsy. Let's move on." I felt the terrible joy of being an asshole, the knowledge I'd gone too far.

"Fuck you. It's like having three kids. Why should I be married to someone who doesn't give a shit?"

"Now you're swearing at me. I don't do that to you."

"And that's tactic two, pick on something about me instead of dealing with the issue we're fighting about. And you wonder why we don't have sex." She strode out of the room. "Don't follow me."

It took everything I had to do as she asked, but the one time we'd visited a marriage counsellor together the advice was for me to *leave her alone after fights*. I hated that she boiled our arguments down to two tactics that I used over and over, even if she happened to be right. I wanted to persuade her that she was wrong, about me and our marriage, and especially her idea that sex was out of the question. During the book launch I barely heard two words of the reading, just sat there fuming as I kept replaying our argument in my head.

When I came back home I asked her if she was willing to talk. She didn't respond, but she didn't leave the room either.

I shuffled the coins in my pocket, which I knew drove Betsy crazy, while gathering my courage to speak.

"Can you tell me why you don't want to have sex anymore?"

She was quiet long enough for me to count to fifteen.

"I need to be able to count on you as my teammate in the family. It feels like you aren't really here with us. Whenever I ask for what I need, you label my concerns as ridiculous and un-reasonable. How can I feel attracted to someone who constantly belittles me and disregards my feelings?" She was crying.

I was shocked by her tears but also by what she said.

"I didn't know . . . I'm really sorry."

She was quiet again.

"I've told you this before, Maurice. A lot of times."

I swallowed hard.

"Give me six months, Betsy. Please. I'll help more around the house, and make lists, I'll do more with the boys." She said nothing. "Honestly." Still nothing. "I'll go see a psychologist." Betsy had been asking me to *get help* for years and I'd always resisted. "What do you say?"

"OK. But I've heard this before."

I sat down on the far side of the couch from her in our TV room, and we watched an episode of "Survivor" together. Neither of us spoke.

——

Later that week I made my first visit to the shrink. She came recommended by someone I trusted in the arts community. But I left the first session completely discouraged, certain the painful hour was futile.

—

My one ray of hope that winter came when I suggested we plan a big family vacation for the following year, and Betsy endorsed the idea. When she was a kid in Virginia, every summer her family rented a beach house on an island off the North Carolina coast. Betsy talked about the experience nostalgically, probably the only time she ever sounded that way to me. I said we should save our money and go there next year, make it a road trip. When our conflicts were unbearable I imagined lying on the beach in the hot sun, with Betsy beside me in a bikini, while the boys frolicked in the surf like exotic sea creatures. I hoped this was not a fantasy, and I booked another session with the shrink.

INVENTING MY FAMILY

I

Another cold Winnipeg spring. It was Mother's Day, four years since Betsy and I had adopted the boys in Ukraine. The wind shivered the elm trees while the four of us walked briskly on the dusty sidewalk. Peter moved in front of me, slowing erratically so I had to avoid treading on his heels. He was nine and his feet were big. Bohdan scampered in front of Betsy, chortling at the birds and the sun and our impending breakfast. I held a shiny pink balloon, the kind you give recovering surgery victims in hospital. Two postcards were taped to the tail and they flapped in the prairie wind.

When we got to the schoolyard we stopped in the middle of the soccer field. The only sound was the wind soughing through the wire fence, the only smell the swollen river a quarter mile away, beyond the trees. No cars passed. I read the first postcard out loud. Bohdan had scrawled his message in large letters, and it had taken a lot of time and Betsy's help for him to write this out:

Dear Mama,
I hope you are doing good at your age. I miss you when
I don't be around you. I am angry at you because you did
not take care of me and I am angry at you because you

did not act like you love me. I am angry at you because
you put me in the orphanage, and I am angry at you because
you did not feed me and you did not brush my teeth.
love love love love love love

Bohdan

When I finished reading Bohdan nodded his head and stared with his deep brown eyes into the distance past my shoulder. "I am angry at her," he said. He did not remember his life before adoption. We had told him the story of how his mother left him and how he went to the orphanage with Peter.

Then Peter read his postcard, which he'd written quite quickly on his own:

Dear Mama, I miss
you a lot, I wish
someday we will
meet, when I am
still young.

Love, Love, Love, Love Peter!!

"You don't feel angry at your mother?" I asked Peter.

"No," he said. His long face was serene. I released the balloon and the chilly breeze and helium pulled it up. It glinted above the brick school, and shrank into blue sky until we could not see the postcards anymore.

Then we walked to the diner on Sherbrook Street for breakfast to celebrate Mother's Day with Betsy. As she talked to the boys about their postcards, my mind drifted to *Paradise Lost*, how the preposition "of" begins the first two lines, how Milton hated rhyme. Peter said something. I nodded vacantly and Betsy said *"Maurice"* sharply and glared at me. Peter said, "I know you think about poetry sometimes, Dad," almost as though he'd read my mind.

Betsy glared at me so hard it felt like a kick in the shins.

Walking home we passed the old stone church on Westminster with the bell-tower that reminds me of the one in *Vertigo*. When I was a kid every Mother's Day began with a church service. Every Sunday did, even when we lived abroad. But although Milton spoke to me now, God was silent. We did not attend church. The only religion in our house since the boys arrived was *Star Wars*. Peter and Bohdan believed fervently that there was good in Darth Vader, the dark father. I hoped they were right.

———

In the evening I called my mother to see if her flowers arrived. She and Dad both got on the telephone. She thanked me for the flowers, then said out of nowhere, "Your father has never liked Mother's Day."

There was a pause, and I said, "Well, he was so young when his mother died. Do you remember much about that, Dad?"

"It was a long way to get to the hospital where she was, more than five kilometres. I think maybe we walked, is that right?" He knew I'd talked to Lil about it.

"Lil says you borrowed bicycles," I said.

"Yes, that makes sense."

"Do you remember anything of what she said the last time you saw her?"

"No."

Mom cleared her throat. "Eric, you told me yourself."

"No, I don't remember a thing," Dad said.

Mom insisted. "You did tell me, Eric. You said you wouldn't fight with your sister."

"Yeah, I guess I did. That's right." This was an old disagreement, and I couldn't tell if Dad was sincere or just wanted to avoid an argument with Mom.

"You know why I hated Mother's Day?" he said.

"Why?" I asked.

"They made us wear these stupid white flowers, carnations I think, in school and in church. Everyone whose mother was dead had to wear a white carnation. If your mother was alive you wore a red one."

"So that started in Germany in 1948?"

"Yes, it must have. And it continued in Canada for a long time. You had to go to church with your white carnation. I hated that."

"Mother's Day is hard for Peter and Bohdan too," I said. "Today we had them write postcards to their birth mother, and then we taped them to a helium balloon and let it fly away." I figured Dad would think this was flaky, but he said nothing.

"Is their birth mother dead?" said Mom. I'd answered this question many times before, but she was much more focused than usual today.

"Possibly. She might be a street person. We don't know. We've told the boys only some of what we've found out."

"Nah ya," said Dad, and Mom yawned. *Nah yah* is what Mennonites say in low German when they're tired or resigned to the fate of the world.

I said goodbye to them and listened to their telephones clicking off the line. My dad, I realized, had for the first time volunteered a shard of his fragmented childhood. He had just given me the gift of a bitter flower named so that I could almost touch it, a white carnation pinned on a little boy's first suit.

—

My fifth monthly session with the shrink took place in May. This time I had something positive to report. The boys and I had watched *Duck Soup* together for the second time and they loved it even more than the first! We laughed like fools at the sight gags, especially Harpo burning the big street vendor's hat and later pretending to be Groucho in the mirror scene. Now the boys were old enough to get the verbal humour too. We had so much fun and it felt great to relax my vigilance and just enjoy them. And to discover that like me they could watch a movie over and over. Betsy liked it too, but not enough for repeated viewings.

The shrink wanted to know if I still shirked on my household chores. Yes, but not as often, and at least I knew when I was doing so. She smiled. The hour ended faster than usual.

Later in the month, at our weekly Wendy's dinner, Jeremy told me that, after three years of floundering from one thing to another in university, he had decided to take a year off. He was surprised when I endorsed his decision to go on a backpacker's tour of Asia with a few of his friends. Over the next eight weeks, we received two postcards from him and regular emails, an unprecedented level of communication. I answered the emails immediately on receipt, short messages about the boys and our daily lives and felt grateful for the connection with him.

The first postcard, addressed to "Mo Peter Bohdan Betsy," came from Cambodge, Cambodia, and showed a Buddhist temple with numerous monkeys scampering in the foreground. The message read: "I think this is the species of monkey that bit me." In an earlier email, Jeremy had told us he'd been bitten by a monkey while visiting the temple and gotten a rabies shot.

The second postcard, a time-lapse photograph of Bangkok's skyline at night featuring the beautiful Chao Phraya River, was addressed to "Betsy Bohdan Peter Mo," which I momentarily worried might be a subtle way of reducing my status as his father. Jeremy's poetically fragmented observation, written in the big childish scrawl that resembled my own, shattered the romantic illusion of the photo:

> *River boats, the only way*
> *of getting around Bangkok*
> · *that doesn't involve*
> *taking your life in your hands, or fill you*
> *with rage.*
>
> *Miss you guys!*
>
> *Love,*
> *Jeremy*

Jeremy was supposed to catch his flight home from Thailand. But in spring 2009 street protests almost shut down Bangkok for the second time in about a year. I clicked the refresh button on the *New York Times* Thailand web page every hour. Jeremy sent an email saying he wasn't sure he'd be able to reach the airport. Betsy contacted a friend who lived in Bangkok, and she drove Jeremy through the city's chaotic back roads to the airport.

When he was back in Winnipeg I noticed the darkening hair on his legs, the receding line of hair on his head just like mine at the same age, the sharp smell of his cologne. I hugged him for the first time in years, just for a moment, and I let go before he did. But it was not a board hug.

——

In our session with the child psychologist, she'd recommended that Peter write a journal, and that we discuss its contents with him. I liked the idea. My parents had encouraged me to keep a diary when I was about ten, and I'd kept one off and on ever since. For the first few years Mom and Dad had insisted I write every day, often correcting my spelling, though we never talked about what I'd written. My childhood entries were distinctly humdrum ("went to school; I hate math"), but occasionally the writing let me blow off steam.

For a while we encouraged Peter to write an entry every day as well, and he dutifully recorded his lack of excitement for the exercise, writing at most a couple of sentences. Then Betsy discovered a diary format in another adoptive mom's blog. It used a fill-in-the-blank formula that began *Today I felt mad,* or *glad,* or *sad and scared when . . .* followed by three lines for each response. Betsy made a binder for Peter with photocopied sheets of these fill-in-the-blank forms so he could write about his feelings every day.

For the next two months Peter cooperated. Much of what he wrote was touching and also hard for us to read:

Today I felt sad when . . . I thought at the start of the day about my first mother, that she left me.

I am thankful for . . . I have strict parents; I have nice parents

Today I felt glad when . . . Dad picked me up at Daycare! I was lonely by myself.

Today I felt scared when . . . dad is going away for five days because people have left me before forever!

3 things I like about myself . . . I have nice skin!; I am handsome; I controlled my anger!; I told the truth today; I was kind

I am thankful . . . to have a kitten; To have a father; To have a mother

Somewhere in his litanies of thankfulness, Peter wrote "I got to watch *Star Wars*. All of it." Peter loved *Star Wars* the way I had loved the Biggles adventure stories as a boy in Jamaica, raiding the colonial library. Biggles was a British spy who did glamorous things that were forbidden to me by my parents or the larger world: he pointed guns at bad guys, he said "damn" and "what the devil," he smoked cigarettes, he flew airplanes, he solved mysteries.

Of course the hero of *Biggles Investigates* and *Biggles Sorts it Out* would have let himself be tortured to death before he ever said, as Luke does to Darth Vader, "Search your feelings, Father." When Peter echoed Luke in his journal, writing "I felt my feelings today," Betsy and I were relieved and hopeful, though I felt like a hypocrite for steering Peter in that direction when I still identified more with Biggles than Luke, and suspected my dad would as well.

———

As a way of getting through to Peter, Betsy wanted me to reveal some of my own *difficult feelings* to the boys. One day at dinner she asked me to tell a story about my first family.

"What first family?" said Bohdan.

"Mom means my family when I lived with your brother Jeremy and Jeremy's mother." I told them a story about Jeremy when he was four, wearing a white sailor outfit and getting his picture taken. I didn't mention trying to kick a car that day because it cut me off as I carried Jeremy out of the photographer's studio.

"He had chubby cheeks and he was ticklish, just like you." No one was satisfied with this story.

"Dad has hurts that he doesn't talk about either," Betsy said, as a prompt for me. We'd talked about how my opening up more in front of the kids might be helpful to them, especially to Peter, but I just wasn't ready. I mumbled and continued to eat my dinner. The boys were distracted by looking at a baby picture of Jeremy that Betsy brought out.

My level of inexpressiveness reminded me again of my father's, and it filled me with dread and anger at myself. As Peter wrote in his diary so often: "Today I felt mad when I had to tell about my feelings."

Every city has an unspoken contract between pedestrians and vehicles that specifies what each party will tolerate from the other. For weeks in the early summer I'd been violating this contract. Instead of meekly letting drivers cut me off at four-way stops while they inched forward into the crosswalk, I continued walking at a uniform speed and thumped the back of their vehicles with my open hand. Usually this elicited hostile stares. Sometimes drivers, invariably male, gave me the finger. I gave it back to them. But there was no satisfaction in this DIY enforcement of the traffic laws. I arrived at home distracted and enraged, unable to face a blank screen or notebook.

One morning at the corner of Wolseley and Evanson, a silver Toyota truck rolled through the stop sign, forcing me to check slightly as I crossed the street. I whacked the side of the truck hard with my hand while continuing to walk to the other side.

The driver pulled over, slammed his door shut, and came charging at me. I'd stopped, filled with caffeinated self-righteousness, and at first noticed only that he was a short man. Then, as he got closer, I saw that he was short and powerfully built.

"What the fuck are you doing?" He was now within inches of me.

"You cut me off. You shouldn't cut off pedestrians." This sounded, even to me, like the whine of someone who types a lot. I looked to see if he was carrying a tire iron while part of me realized that it was too late for such worries.

"Ffffuh. . ." he bellowed, not a word but just pure anger, and then his hands were on my throat. He rocked me back and forth. I could see the shaving nicks on his face now, and felt the callouses on his hands. I'd never been in a fight. I had no idea what to do other than stand up straight, because I clung to the notion that my height was an advantage, and I knew that I shouldn't let him put me on the ground. But my hands stayed at my sides.

"Get off me. I've memorized your licence number," I squeaked out, my voice reedy.

He grunted and let go, flinging his hands down to his sides with disgust, and headed to his truck. A wave of violated dignity and relief rushed through me.

"I'm calling the cops. You attacked me."

"You do that," he said, with his back to me, getting into the small truck without ducking his squat body. I stood still at the corner and watched him drive down the street and turn, probably to a construction site just around the corner. My hands shook and at home I stared at a dark bruise forming above my collarbone.

———

I called Betsy at work and told her what had happened. I omitted telling her how often I'd been smacking vehicles, how angry I'd been before and afterward, how humiliated I felt after this last encounter. I admitted being scared. She asked me to describe the vehicle in detail.

It was Betsy's day to pick up the boys after school, and on the way there she found the silver Toyota and methodically deflated the tires, based on the description I'd rattled off.

"What if someone saw you, Mom?" said Peter when she told the story at dinner. He and Bohdan had listened with close attention. They were awed and impressed by the vandalism, that their straight-arrow mother had done it, and filled with the spirit of self-righteous indignation that had caused the incident in the first place.

"Dad did something dangerous, and so did I," said Betsy. While she told the story I'd felt a moment of gratitude and love. And yet I was also ungrateful.

—

I told the whole story to the members of my poetry workshop, who were all women, and they thought it was *cute*. It showed how *devoted* Betsy was to me. But all I could think of was that Betsy had played the hero, Biggles to my colonial flunky, and that the boys, who had once thought I could lift up a car single-handed, had transferred that hero-worship to their mother. I kept imagining what it would have been like for the boys to see me clench my fists and glare at the truck driver so he scurried away, unable to touch me.

II

At home in my study, I stared out the window, watching for the hunched-up old lady in a black shroud who hobbled down the street at three o'clock every afternoon with her middle-aged daughter.

It was late June, and I was trying to write a review of a book I didn't like. The author had once written good books, but now wrote imitations of himself from that earlier period. How to say this? How to make myself care about the diplomacy for less than $50?

As the school day wound down I always felt anxious. At age seven, Bohdan rarely had problems in school, although he had contributed to my worries before: in grade one he and a classmate urinated all over the walls of the washroom, and they also tried flushing a basketball down the toilet; in grade two Bohdan pushed the same boy's head into a brick wall as part of an argument.

Now nine, Peter frequently had problems in school, in ways that were sometimes predictable and other times surprised me. If I was leaving town, or we were about to go on vacation, or for no discernible reason, Peter might have an incident that would trigger a phone call from the principal: he had opened up filing cabinets containing confidential student records and rifled through them; he'd inserted bent paper clips into electrical outlets in his classroom; he'd stolen food from the special refrigerator reserved for the teachers. Both Peter and Bohdan had behavioural reporting systems with their teachers. Peter got a number between one and five, with five being an excellent day. He lost a privilege when the number fell below four, and gained one from four up. Bohdan's teacher wrote a paragraph describing his day.

At 3:15 the computer alarm reminded me to gear up for the boys' return. I began my *gearing up* ritual by listening to a Bill Evans tune from his early period, something with the distinctly classical sound that I liked, clinical and intensely emotional, like Glenn Gould playing the Goldberg Variations. Sometimes I stretched and breathed slowly while listening. After that I usually recited the Twenty-Third Psalm to myself, or a poem; my shrink had recommended recordings by a mindfulness guru with a squeaky, grating voice, so I'd invented my own exercises.

I checked the weather in Emerald Isle, North Carolina, and imagined what the beach would be like in July next year.

The point of this routine was to make myself calm and receptive. My shrink said I needed to react in less volatile ways, to not let myself be provoked into losing my temper, either by a bad behaviour report from a teacher, or Peter's mood, or his deliberate attempts at provocation. My father had always become cold when he was angry at me, but I waxed hot. Now I wanted to be *mindful*.

On this particular day I listened to Evans playing "Someday My Prince Will Come," then stretched rather quickly because I hated stretching. The telephone rang.

It was the principal. Peter had just gotten out of her office. He had apparently threatened to cut another boy's face with a paper clip. This boy had been following Peter around the schoolyard before the incident. Peter asked him to go away, but he didn't.

I asked the principal if it was a certain kid who'd been bothering Peter recently, taunting him until he reacted and came home with a bad report.

She said she knew that Peter had been bullied by this boy, which I was glad to hear. But I agreed that we'd talk to Peter about threatening other kids.

The side door opened. "Hi Dad!" It was Bohdan, loud, bouncing off the wall, almost falling down the steep basement stairs.

"Hi Bohdan. How was your day?"

"Good!"

"All right. Get your backpack emptied."

A moment later Peter walked in. I greeted him and he turned away.

"Peter, let's go talk in your room. Bohdan, you should get your snack ready."

Peter and I sat on his bed. I put my hand on his shoulder and he shrugged it off. "Tell me what happened."

"Max and another boy laughed at me. They followed me around." Peter had to stop here because he was taking retching gasps of air and crying. "I went outside and they kept following me."

"Did you tell them to leave you alone?"

"Yes I did. I was nice about it too. Max wouldn't listen." Peter lost his voice again. "I was on the play structure and Max laughed at me. I held up a paper clip and told him not to come any closer."

"Did you threaten to cut Max with the clip?" I had to repress a smile.

"No. No. I told the principal I never said anything."

"You know what Max is doing to you, Peter?"

"What?" He let me put my arm around him.

"He wants you to get in trouble. So he bugs you and bugs you until you react in a way that he can tattle. It's really hard but you can't lose your temper and threaten him by waving something around, not even a paper clip."

"It's not fair," sobbed Peter.

"Listen. I believe you that you never said you'd cut him. But you can't threaten anyone by making a gesture, even a kid who's a total jerk. Something is hurt inside Max that makes him scared, so he behaves like an asshole. By the way you can't use that language outside our house, but Max is an asshole. Doesn't matter though — you still can't threaten him, otherwise you'll be the one who gets in trouble. And you're right, it isn't fair." He leaned into me and relaxed, sobbing the whole time. I couldn't protect him from whatever lurked in his past but I could hold him for now. It made me feel the same rush of fiercely protective love that I'd felt when we first met, when he had his Frankenstein bandage on his forehead and the baby fat still in his face.

A few days later, I got another call from school, this time about Bohdan. He'd hit his head on a bookshelf, and might need stitches.

"How are you doing?" I said when he came out to me in the hall.

"You can die from a cut in the head," he said. "If you die, then you go to be with God."

"Where did you hear that?"

Bohdan shrugged. "You go to be with God, in the God-place."

"You mean heaven?"

"Yes, to heaven. Unless you get shotted twice. Then you stay buried in the ground, dead."

"Why don't you go to heaven if you're shot twice?"

"You can only get shotted once." I nodded and we set off to see the doctor.

Late in the afternoon we went by the daycare centre to pick up Peter. He'd heard what happened to Bohdan and was happy to see us. Bohdan was happy too. He hadn't needed any stitches, just a bit of skin glue, and I'd bought him some candy to celebrate his good luck. The prospect of a concussion still worried me. But for the moment I was happy to have the boys safe beside me.

"Look at the sky," I said to them. "Look at the beautiful blue sky, and the moon."

"I don't see the moon," said Bohdan.

"Look," said Peter, pointing. "Just above the trees. You can see the craters!"

"And do you see how beautiful the sky is?"

"Yes," they both said. We walked home fast in the cold air.

When we got home I decided to tell Peter and Bohdan the story of my grandfather's death. It didn't make much sense, and maybe they were too young to hear it, but I needed to tell them. It was a story I wished my dad had told me early in my life. Maybe my sons would see how much they shared with their grandfather, even though our birth families were not the same and they saw him only once a year.

"He was the father of my father, your grandpa's dad. He was killed by the government, by the police," I said. "He was shot."

"Why would police kill him?" asked Peter.

"Bad people ran the government. He was a Mennonite, which means he believed in God and spoke German. The government didn't like that."

"Why not?" said Bohdan.

"They wanted everyone to just believe in the leader whose name was Stalin. My grandfather lived in a country called the Soviet Union that no longer exists. Where they lived, where your grandpa was born, is now Ukraine."

"So Grandpa is Ukrainian, like us?" said Peter.

"Yes."

I didn't tell them that my grandfather was like the hamster in Bohdan's room, incapable of leaving the cage they put him in, or the cage of his own beliefs. He could have run from the authorities and maybe stayed alive at least for a while. But God was like alcohol for him, a substance that changed the chemistry of his brain, an illness.

I did tell them that Grandpa had lost his parents too; like them he was an orphan, and also like them he ended up with a loving family. I said that Grandpa had trouble talking about his feelings as well. Finding words for the pain you feel is hard.

III

It is striking how often earliest memories are painful ones. "Maurice is upset about any little noise — he's afraid of bombs," my father wrote in his diary in 1967, when we lived in Nigeria. I was five.

Dad had built a sandbox beside the driveway. I played in it with my Lego blocks and toy cars for hours every day under the shade of a huge flamboyant tree. Sometimes Dad helped me arrange the flamboyant seeds into roads, airports, a parliament, and my sister Crisy messed them up.

One day jets flew low overhead, and they didn't look like the planes we took to Nigeria. At dinner I asked my father about them. He said they were air force planes. They were flying to Biafra to drop bombs and shoot people because Nigeria was at war with Biafra.

At night I thought about the planes, their menace. They were not like the soldiers, who were cheerful and friendly, waving at the roadside. At checkpoints the soldiers might have low, harsh voices, but then Dad gave them money and joked with them, using a few words in their language, and they were cheerful again. The planes were supposed to bomb people in Biafra, but what if they bombed us by mistake?

Now when I played in the sandbox I looked up at the sky every few minutes, or cocked my ear for the rushing sounds of their engines. When the planes flew over, I ran to the bathroom and latched the door on a place full of flies and bad smells, but it felt safe until the horrible noise went away.

When Jeremy was five, he and I drove for ten straight hours in a green Honda Civic from Winnipeg to southern Saskatchewan for a family gathering, taking only short breaks every two hours for bathroom, snacks, and caffeine. My mother's family had rented a big A-frame cabin for the weekend in the Cypress Hills near Swift Current. The morning after our arrival about ten of us went for a walk in the scrub pine off the road. Jeremy liked to stamp around on his shoes, demonstrating his mastery of the ground beneath him. Somehow he stepped on a wasp nest under a rotting log and within seconds had been stung multiple times. He cried loudly and the bites swelled as I raced him to the Swift Current hospital, terrified he might be allergic. The stings and swellings are the only part of the day he remembers.

—

Peter had no conscious memories before the orphanage, but he'd told us about a dream that seemed to go further back.

In Peter's dream he was in a house with his mother on the second floor. He was not sure if Bohdan was there too. She approached him from behind as he sat.

"She wants to hug me every time I try crawling toward her, but then she runs or jumps into the air and vanishes," Peter said. "When I try to get a glimpse of her face it always disappears. When I'm in range to see her face it fades. I just see lots of colours and then she fades."

"It sounds like a digital eraser," I said.

"Yes, so I couldn't see what her face was like." Then, Peter said, she signalled with her hands *no don't come closer*. She wagged her finger at him. When his mother spoke again she said she had to go but would be right back. She went down the stairs.

"Where are you when she leaves?" I asked.

"I don't know. Somewhere so I can't move. But she's a liar," Peter said, stomping his foot for emphasis, his chin wobbling as if it had been rolled in gravel. "She doesn't ever come back."

He sat on my lap and his shoulders heaved.

———

My father's first memory was the mass murder of people he later discovered were Jews. He told me he could remember only this one image of German soldiers shooting the people into a mass grave, but Lil told me that she remembered an officer running upstairs with his face contorted. He said that he'd had it with *this work, diese Arbeit*. But down below the willing executioners kept doing their duty. And after it was over people from the village picked up the coats the Jews had been forced to abandon.

———

As a teenager, the first poem I memorized was a fragment from Alfred Lord Tennyson's *In Memoriam*:

I sometimes hold it half a sin
To put in words the grief I feel;
For words, like Nature, half reveal
and half conceal the Soul within.

But, for the unquiet heart and brain,
A use in measured language lies;
The sad mechanic exercise,
Like dull narcotics, numbing pain.

My grade ten English teacher said the poem was about the death of Tennyson's best friend, and ignored my question about whether Lord T had used drugs.

I knew a deep well of pain lay in my father's childhood, a grief that he could not speak. Fear and pain, also half concealed and largely beyond words, lingered in Peter's unquiet brain. Jeremy felt the sting of my leaving his mother's house when he was twelve, a more profound pain than those wasps. And Bohdan did not remember anything before he met us, but his occasional rages revealed his early, pre-linguistic acquaintance with the grief of abandonment as well.

My own grief had shallower roots than my father's or my sons', yet I was the one exploring their earliest memories. Peter did not do so in his diary, nor had my father in his autobiography. I was the one stuck in the past, sifting through words, while Betsy moved forward with Peter and Bohdan. The only way to numb my pain was to keep writing this book, to try to catch up with my family by typing.

IV

Late in the summer of 2009, Betsy and I decided to tell the boys everything we knew about their family in Ukraine. The child psychologist had advised us to answer all their questions about their mother and family as soon as we thought feasible, but it was a hard decision to make.

The first letter that Olga — the Ukrainian investigator we'd hired in 2007 — sent us began with this tactful introduction:

> *I understand that it is better to read nice words but I think that you should know the truth. . . . You made a decision and I hope that you are ready and you would like to know everything. . . . I hope that it will help you to understand the situation better.*

Betsy and I had not been shocked by the information her letter revealed; some of it contradicted what Oleg told us, but we had always known that Oleg had a compromised relationship with the truth. The boys were seven and nine now, and we agreed that Betsy would tell them the story. I would have begun to weep and mix up the details. I trusted Betsy to tell it the right way, the way parents in religious households trust the Christmas story in Luke.

The four of us sat on the front porch at our new picnic table. Betsy had cut her hair short, like her mother's had been, with the same dark, fierce curls. She made eye contact with each of the boys and then told them. We wanted them to know more about their own history, their surviving relatives, their birth parents, and their medical history, and we'd hired someone to help us find out. Peter, who often preferred the beautiful lie to the difficult truth, started to squirm uncomfortably in his seat.

"The woman we hired, her name was Olga," said Betsy. "She took the train all the way from Kyiv to the west of the country, where your family lived."

"How long did it take her to ride the train?" asked Peter, eager to distract us into details.

"About eight hours. We took that same train when we first met you and Bohdan. Olga went to the province where you lived. In Ukraine the provinces are called oblasts."

"I like that name," said Peter.

"It's a nice name," Betsy responded. "So Olga went to the village where we knew your brother Viktor lived. She asked people where he was and they referred her to one house in the village. There Olga found a woman chopping firewood. She was short and her clothes were dirty and shabby. Olga asked her about your brother Viktor. She answered that he wasn't home.

"That woman is your aunt Inna, and Viktor's too. She is the sister of your birth mother. Aunt Inna's house was where your family lived. Your grandparents lived there too."

"And did she find my mother?" asked Peter. Bohdan was fidgeting with his legs under the table as if he'd rather be someplace else.

"Just wait for Mom to finish, Peter," I said.

"This is what Olga found out about your birth mother, whose name was Nadja. She finished her education at the village school and left home. She didn't want to get a job or continue with more education. She met a man named Roman and they had three children: Viktor, who was born in 1984, a sister Jane in 1985, and another brother Dima in 1986. 1986 is the same year Jeremy was born."

"Our brothers are just as big as Jeremy?" said Bohdan, looking up from his legs.

"Yes, Olga said they're the same size," I said. "Just as tall, so you guys will probably be tall too." Height mattered to me.

"Then your mother left on her own, without her children. Your grandparents raised the kids. Your aunt Inna has not seen her sister, your birth mother, for at least ten years. Aunt Inna is not very sure of dates because she does not read or write much."

"That's sad!" said Bohdan.

"She knows your birth mother did not come to her parents' funerals. Some people in the village have seen her in the city of Ternopil. They say she lives on the street."

"I can't believe that's true," said Peter, argumentatively.

"I know this is really hard for you, Peter." Betsy stroked his shoulder. "But there's more to tell." Peter nodded.

"After your mother had her first three children, she met another man and had two more babies: Petro and Bogdan, you and your brother. She couldn't take care of children so she left you with her first husband Nikolai. Then later you lived with Aunt Inna in the village. Aunt Inna is poor. She works on a farm as a milkmaid but she doesn't get paid."

"Why don't they pay her?" said Peter.

"Sometime Dad can tell you more about the history of Ukraine. They are a poor country, especially the farmers. Anyway, Aunt Inna doesn't get much help from her husband, because he is an alcoholic and lets her do all the work. They have five children."

"But where is our mom?"

"Peter, no one knows. People from her village have seen her, but not for a few years."

"Is she dead?"

"She might be. We just don't know."

"Why can't we write her a letter?"

"She doesn't have an address or a telephone number. She might be homeless."

Peter buried his face in his hands and collapsed on the table. Bohdan continued to fidget. I put my arm on Peter's shoulder.

"Your brother Viktor was in the hospital when Olga was there," Betsy continued. "His leg was cut off and he needed to get an artificial one." Now Bohdan looked up, legs still. He was always interested in gory accidents.

"Who cut off his leg?" said Bohdan.

"He got hurt in an accident on the farm. He was probably caught between the tractor and some other equipment," I said.

"We don't even know that much," said Betsy, never willing to speculate. "It was a farm accident where he drove a tractor and the wound was infected. He got gangrene and they cut off the leg."

"Was he on crutches?" Bohdan asked.

"Yes, he was. We'll show you a picture."

"Can we see it now?" asked Bohdan eagerly.

"No. We'll show you in a minute." Betsy said. We had decided to tell them the story before they saw the pictures Olga had emailed us. "Your brother Viktor works hard. He fixes appliances, TV sets, tape recorders, whatever people have in the village."

"Are there pictures of my mother?" Bohdan wanted to know.

"Olga asked your brother if he had pictures of the family but he doesn't. He did have pictures of your mom, but he burnt them all up."

"Why did he do that?" said Bohdan. Peter still had his head down.

"He was angry at his mother because she left him. In the letter Olga writes that he said, 'If she doesn't need me I don't need her.'" Bohdan nodded. He understood anger. "Your aunt Inna doesn't have any pictures either. Her life is hard. She does not even know the birthdates of her children."

"Why? Doesn't she have a calendar?" asked Peter, taking his head off the table.

"She probably did not get much education," I said. "She maybe can't read a calendar, even if she had the money to buy one." Olga had told us that 'Inna is a very rural person,' a euphemism I guessed for all kinds of misery.

"Your aunt says that her daughter has the same fingernail and toenail shapes as you guys do," said Betsy. "They are just like your mother's, and your aunt thought it was funny that you all have the same shape too."

"Why didn't she keep us?" asked Peter, his face rigid and serious.

"She had to let you and Bohdan go to the orphanage because there wasn't enough food for all the kids."

Peter's head was back on the table, and Betsy stroked it as he said, "I can't believe she's homeless. I try to imagine her out there, sometimes I dream of her, and . . ." His shoulders shook with an indelible, unshakeable pain. My eyes blurred and refracted the scene through a kind of prism: Peter collapsing under the weight of what Betsy and I thought he needed to know; Jeremy fleeing the room when his mother and I announced our divorce, another death; my dad struggling to keep his grief at his mother's fate closed off even from himself.

In August I began playing some opera for the boys on my turntable on the weekends and at dinner. We got *Carmen* on DVD from the library and the boys loved watching it. Neither of them questioned the idea that people might sing instead of talk, often about their deepest feelings and, especially while dying, at great length. Then one Saturday Peter and I went to a movie theatre to see the Metropolitan Opera broadcast. I'd decided Bohdan was too young for the three hours of *Il Trovatore*.

Peter was enthusiastic. I warned him about how long it would be, and how you had to stay quiet in your seat. I read him the plot description for Act I and he said *it's too much*, he'd figure it out while he watched. It was the same problem I'd always had with *Il Trovatore* myself. It was too much. And even once you kept the plot straight there was the challenge of keeping a straight face. A bitter gypsy woman so bent on avenging her mother that she mistakenly throws her own baby boy into the fire instead of the evil count's son, and then raises the accidentally spared scion of the dark count lovingly, as her own? But the music transcends the mounting implausibilities.

The broadcast began with a shot of the Met's interior: glittering balconies full of shiny people, then the main level even more iridescent, all the women blonde, all the men in black tie.

"Why are the lights on?" said Peter.

"Because we're watching a live broadcast of an opera from New York, and they'll turn the lights off here at the same time they do over there. You know when Grandpa was a boy he watched the Metropolitan Opera when they came on tour here to Winnipeg."

"Wouldn't it be better if they still came here?" Peter asked.

"Yes, it would."

Then we were launched into Act I. During the duel Peter gripped the side of his chair. Count di Luna stalked around singing that he was full of fury, very angry. The singer had shock-white hair and snarled sideways, his mouth almost foaming with rage.

At the intermission we waited for the on-screen clock to tell us how much time we had, and then headed to the lobby, where I gave Peter the granola bar and apple we'd brought from home, hidden under our jackets.

"Wouldn't it be great to just sing when you got really mad?" I asked Peter.

"Yes," he said.

"Are you enjoying the opera?"

"Yes." He wanted to try one of the video games in the movie theatre's gigantic lobby. He had no spending money but managed to scavenge a single token left in a machine, not enough to actually play. I ate my granola bar, and watched him pretend to play a *Star Wars* shoot-'em-up until the call to return to the theatre.

We took our seats for the third act, Peter again gripping his seat when Manrico sang his vow to *rescue his mother*, the revenge-obsessed gypsy. I suddenly thought of my dad, and wondered if he'd wanted to rescue his mother on that beautiful spring day in 1945 that he barely remembers. And what about Peter? Wouldn't he love to rescue his mother? Manrico sprinted up the massive stairs of the turntable set, and I was in tears.

Every aria, every musical gesture at all over the next half hour made me dribble more tears. I found a tissue in my leather jacket and dabbed at my cheeks and glasses. I wanted revenge for my grandmother, for Peter's mother, vengeance on the forces of poverty and ignorance. I wanted revenge for those women crying in Syria, in Sudan, in Rwanda, in the Balkans, for every mother in the world. I glanced, embarrassed, at Peter in the half-lit theatre. He was too immersed in the opera to notice my tears, and by the time the lights went up I was once again in control of myself.

"What was your favourite part?" I asked as we walked to the car. He thought for a minute.

"When Leonora came to the prison and sang for a long time about how she loves him." And he tucked his hand into mine.

A week later he told me his favourite part was the execution and the gypsy's revenge, when she told the count he'd killed his brother. I was struck by Peter's ability to hold all these impulses at once: his admiration for Leonora, his desire for revenge, and his angry longing for justice in a world where people die every day just like Manrico did. As for the music, he said, "I loved all the music. It blurs together in my mind. It's like eating too much. You're happy and you're sad." I loved Peter then, more fiercely than I ever had before.

—

The wind rushed through the elm trees and the cottonwoods as Peter and I walked down our block to the corner grocery, smelling the last dry heat of summer that promises to never leave.

"That TV show last night," he said, "is that true?" The show had been about hypnosis.

"Yes, it was true, it was a documentary. Do you know the word *mesmerize*?"

"Yes, Dad."

"It comes from a Dr. Mesmer who invented hypnosis. And Sigmund Freud, who invented modern psychology, he used hypnosis for a while too. People are still hypnotized now so they can stop smoking." Peter took this in.

"Could there be a speaker under your bed at night, and it tells you and Mom *give Peter his DS back* over and over while you sleep, so you do it?" Recently we'd confiscated Peter's Nintendo DS because he played with it in his bedroom after lights out.

"That won't work, Peter."

"Why not?" He giggled, then held my hand, suddenly serious. "Since hypnosis can help people to stop smoking, could it help me not think about stealing?"

"I didn't know you thought about stealing anymore." To my knowledge Peter had not stolen since the previous year, when he was eight.

"Sometimes I do think about it."

"Well, with smoking the patient has to be willing to stop for the hypnotic suggestions to work. I'm not willing to give you your Nintendo back right now, and your thoughts about stealing are probably too complicated for hypnosis."

I sketched Freud's idea of the unconscious for him while he looked at passing traffic, squirrels, kids rolling on the grass in front of their houses. But I knew he was listening.

"Freud gave up on hypnosis," I said, "because he worried about patients having relapses. A relapse is when you fall back into something. Is that what you're worried about with stealing?"

"Yes, I guess so. I think about my birth mom and get upset. The pain is so strong I can't stand it, like staring at the sun."

"Do you think maybe you feel sad because you can't protect your birth mom, or rescue her like Manrico in the opera?"

"How about if a psychologist hypnotized me," said Peter, not answering directly, "and then while I was mesmerized, they got me to say: everything will be fine. Your mother did not abandon you because she hated you. She really loved you."

"I wish it was that easy, Peter." And I really did. We walked the rest of the way in silence. The morning glories were in full bloom on Westminster and the sun pulsed beautiful and frightening.

It had been three months since I wrote the psychologist the one last cheque. The sessions had seemed pointless, though I had to admit that my relationship with Betsy was changing in small but discernible ways. Betsy still did nearly all the meal preparation, and though I disappeared into my study on the third floor to write, I emerged in time to tidy the kitchen before she got home. Nor did I complain about being the courier of large and small objects in our house, which entailed running up and down four flights of stairs to fetch items never in the most convenient place. I talked with the boys more easily, and took an active part in discussions at the dinner table now. Also, I started weekend chore lists myself, emptied the dishwasher without any reminders, and even inspected the dishes for food particles before putting them away. Small things. Though like Peter I did have relapses.

I had also started taking each of the boys out for a father-son dinner once a month. A few weeks after the opera I took Peter to a vegetarian restaurant on Sherbrook Street. Peter loved food in a deep and sensual way, and he had an adaptable palate. That evening he ordered a barbecue-flavoured veggie burger.

"You know the opera we saw, *Il Trovatore?*" I asked him as the summer sun poured down on us. He looked up from eating to nod. "Do you know what part made me cry?"

"Yes. When the man wants to rescue his mother."

"How on earth did you know that?"

He shrugged.

"Do you know why?"

Peter shook his head. His mouth was full of veggie fries that he ate too fast, and his face smeared with organic ketchup from a bright red bottle that said Made in New Jersey.

"When the hero, Manrico, sings about rescuing his mother, it made me cry because I thought of you and Grandpa both wanting to rescue your mothers. Don't you wish you could rescue your mother?"

Peter responded with his own questions. "Why would Grandpa want to rescue his mother? She died when he was my age, right?"

"Yes, she did. Peter," I touched his shoulder and lowered my voice, "you don't want everyone to hear you, so you need to lower your volume." Recently Peter had been close to shouting in most conversations, especially when he was excited.

"Grandpa's mom died when he was a boy, you're right. But I've never told you before about how she was raped by soldiers during the war." Peter shook his head and his eyes filled with tears. "That's what Grandpa would want to rescue his mother from," I said and took a breath, realizing that I should probably stop on this subject. "And don't you wish you could rescue your mother sometimes?"

"Yes, I do. But I don't understand why people do things like that in a war."

"You mean rape? Please sit up, Peter." I was worried the organic ketchup would go all over his white T-shirt.

"Yes. And Grandpa's mom wasn't even in the army."

"In war sometimes the point is just to make the enemy suffer, and the enemy includes everyone who is different from you."

"Maybe the men who did that had their own hurts and difficult feelings."

"I'm sure they did. Anyway, I want to talk about how it affected Grandpa." He looked down and turned pale in the sturdy sunshine. "Don't worry, I'm not going to tell the story of what happened exactly." He looked up at me.

"Grandpa can remember all kinds of things from the day his mother was attacked. He remembers how the yard looked, what kind of trees they had, how a plane flew over, how the soldiers tossed a grenade into the pond just to watch the dead fish float to the surface." At this Peter shook his head in short spasmodic movements, very upset.

"But Grandpa doesn't remember what happened to his mother. He was eight years old, only two years younger than you are. So he was old enough to remember, not like you with your mother. Why do you think he doesn't remember?"

"I say it's because your brain is like a computer when you push control-alt-delete. You restart and then you don't remember. Or you put the thoughts away and they're like an apple core in the compost." Peter loved metaphors and analogies.

"But the apple core just becomes dirt again. What about your thoughts or memories? Do they disappear like something in the computer's memory might?"

"No, no they don't." He ate some more fries.

"Then you didn't answer my question before. Why doesn't Grandpa remember what happened to his mom?"

"Maybe it's too hard to think about for him."

"Yes. I believe that's true. What kinds of worries do you think he had about his family after his mom died?"

"He probably always worried about losing his relatives, about losing people. He maybe thought, who will die next? Just like if someone tried to attack Bohdan, or my parents, or you, my brain would tell my body, *you have to fight!*" This last in a loud declamation; I gave him my lower-the-volume hand signal. "You know how people can get superhuman powers when they're in emergencies, so they can even lift cars? That would happen to me. I'd bite and kick and not let anyone attack us."

"I'm sure you'd fight hard." Enough reality for one dinner, I thought, remembering how Peter and Bohdan once believed in my superhuman powers.

"Dad, you should talk to Grandpa so he doesn't worry about losing Grandma."

"Grandma isn't dying. She's losing her memory."

"Yes, but that's like she's dying inside, and probably it scares Grandpa. You should talk to him. He must be worried about his family leaving him, just like I am."

"It's different with your dad when he's older. He wouldn't want me presuming to understand him." I ground to a halt. Hadn't I just been assuming I understood Peter?

"You should talk to Grandpa," Peter said, ignoring my excuse-making. I nodded and he insisted that I finish his burger. The barbecue flavour was extraordinary.

The next day I took Peter's advice and telephoned my father in Edmonton. But rather than inquire into his feelings, I asked him to tell me again the story of how he almost drowned. He did not hesitate.

"We lived near the Dutch border in Germany. I was ten and my mother was still alive. I was playing on an icy pond."

At the edges, the bare branches of the chestnut trees swayed in the wind, just like they used to around the pond on his stepfather's estate.

"I loved the water — this was the pond where I learned to swim in the summer."

Dad had taught himself to swim by pretending he could already do it; it was no more dangerous than running away from drunken, trigger-happy soldiers.

"I was sliding across the ice and felt cracks rippling behind me. When I looked down I could see fish swimming. They were blue."

On this winter day, men were nearby sawing fresh-cut lumber. They must have cut a hole in the ice earlier, and it had frozen over. Dad stepped on the thin ice and suddenly fell in — wet socks, wet shoes, wet pants, and no air. The sheer cold choked his lungs. Where was the hole? The blue sky gone now and he saw only shades of white. But then he saw a dark shape above the ice, moving.

"I kicked hard with my legs, and got my arms out of the water, then I hoisted myself on my elbows to get my head up, and lunged at the dark shape."

A log had stopped just beside the hole like a curling rock. His hand slid over the gnarly surface and caught on an irregular bump. He pulled himself onto the ice and lay there for a moment, his clothes drooping beside him.

Then he went home and was drying himself by the fire when his mother came home from her job. When she asked what happened, he refused to tell her, and she spanked him.

"She was very strict." He couldn't remember what she spanked him with that time or how hard she had hit him.

My hearing this story probably wasn't what Peter had in mind when he told me to talk to my father. But Dad's telling me the story meant a great deal to me, given his sparse writings. Like my father's, Peter's diaries revealed very little, and that didn't bother me. But maybe in his seventies, when he felt safe enough, Peter would tell his son or daughter a story like my dad's.

—

In November I drove to Regina to do a poetry reading in the midst of a crisis. Bohdan's cat, Gracie Flames, had disappeared for several days. Over the weekend we'd walked the streets calling her, phoned the humane society and the no-kill shelters, and put up posters throughout the neighbourhood. Gracie was only a year old and we loved her. Bohdan was distraught.

On the highway, I alternated between Glenn Gould and the Beatles to keep myself awake for the tedious six-hour drive. Downtown Regina had more bustle and tall buildings than it used to. I met my host at a bar and we exchanged books, ate dinner, drank beer. Recently beer had become the thing I liked best about readings. I normally enjoyed these events, happily ignoring the fact that the only people who attend poetry readings are, in declining numerical order, would-be poets, other poets, and friends or relatives. But recently the airless confines of the readings had worn on me. Was there any point to being away from my family for these things? On the other hand, when I was at home I still frequently fought with my wife and lost my temper at Peter.

The reading was held in a tony downtown café with outrageously priced drinks and food. I sold a handful of books and stayed up until 3:00 am at my host's apartment playing crokinole and talking poetry.

The drive home the next morning required more coffee than usual. I left at seven and drove into a fiery sunrise and the astonishing open sky of southern Saskatchewan. I was back in Winnipeg in time to pick the boys up from school.

In the early evening as Bohdan and I left for his tae kwon do class, Gracie limped onto our front walk from the side of the house, and Bohdan picked her up and brought her inside. One of her rear legs was injured and she was extremely thirsty. I took her to the vet the next day.

Her leg was shattered at the hip, probably from the impact of a car. Gracie had always crossed streets with regal indifference. Now she needed surgery and it would cost thousands of dollars.

Betsy and I decided to have Gracie euthanized. We lied to Bohdan, telling him that she died on the operating table. He accepted this news stoically but cried that night. Then he organized a memorial.

We stood around our dining room table where Bohdan had made me light a single candle and he turned out the light. He said we must all hold hands.

"Let's each talk," he said. "We are here to remember my cat Gracie Flames. She was beautiful with her orange flames. She had a happy life being outside a lot. Now she will go back to the earth." He nodded at Peter to follow him.

"January will be very sad. He was Gracie's only brother and this will be hard on him."

"It's OK if you're upset, Peter," said Betsy, squeezing his hand. A tear formed on his cheek. Bohdan pointed at Betsy.

"We will all miss Gracie. We're sad about her dying."

Then it was my turn. I cleared my throat. "We live in a world where a lot of things don't make any sense." I paused and gathered myself. "Gracie's death made no sense. She was a great cat. We miss her a lot."

Bohdan had us close our eyes and think about Gracie for a minute. When we opened our eyes he blew out the candle on the table and we stood in the dark. Where he got this sense of ceremony was a mystery. Peter still had his eyes closed, as if in prayer. Betsy put her arms around me, and then we hugged the boys before Bohdan turned on the light.

VI

In the late spring of 2010, Peter, Bohdan, and I walked home from daycare, just after 5:00 pm. Our usual route was Palmerston, the last street alongside the Assiniboine River. The houses jumbled on different sized lots in a queer variety. It was sleepy and peaceful. An orange tabby crossed our path and stopped to watch us. Bohdan wanted to chase the cat, but I held him back. The sun dappled the sidewalk and each band of light made the street quieter.

"You know," said Peter, in the booming voice he often used, "I don't want to be *attractive* anymore."

"I'm not sure what you mean. You don't want to look nice anymore?" I was wary because Peter often liked to roll out new vocabulary before he understood it.

"It's the way some people have hard corners and others have soft ones — I don't want to be hard. That's attractive. It hurts other people." His voice was loud enough to disturb the orange tabby, who skittered away.

"Peter, what you mean is you don't want to be *destructive*. And the expression is having hard *edges*, not corners." I used my calm and reasonable parent voice.

"No, I *mean* I don't want to be *attractive*."

Bohdan was pulling at my arm, showing me where the cat went.

"You're shouting. Can you explain what you're trying to say, Peter?"

"Well, Dad, have you read *Artemis Fowl*, Dad, the second book?" He repeated *Dad* like this when I most needed to stay calm.

"No. Please just tell me what you're trying to say."

"OK. If I don't listen to you after daycare, and you get mad, and I still don't listen, and you yell at me, that's *attractive*."

"The word you mean is *destructive*. It means something with qualities that destroy."

"But Dad, that's not how I use the words. I say *attractive* for what you're talking about."

"Peter, you can't use words as if they have a private meaning just for you. Words are supposed to be things we use to communicate with others. You can't have a private definition."

"Yes I can."

I sighed. "Look Peter. Do you want other people to understand what you say?" He shrugged, seeing the blind alley he was headed into.

"Peter, I know you want to communicate with other people. There was a German philosopher who talked about this. He said that language by definition is not private. The word you want is *destructive*. *Attractive* means having qualities that attract or draw people to you, such as being good-looking, which you and your brother are, by the way." End of lecture on Wittgenstein, cue self-esteem talk from the most pompous father in the universe, I thought, squeezing Bohdan's hand tighter as Peter spun off on his own. When I asked him again, later that day, Peter remained unwilling to relinquish his private definition of the word *attractive*.

Not only pompous, but hypocritical, I too had my own definition of *attractive*, and it included having dramatic and destructive qualities; this was something I could never admit to Peter. Betsy's definition of attractiveness, she said, included how I stacked shovels, talked to the boys, and put away the dishes in the drainer. I went along, because until I was attractive to her again nothing else mattered to me, and I pinned my hopes like a dead butterfly on our vacation in North Carolina that summer. But some days I felt like a victim of her unreasonable demands. I believed in reason, which was why I liked giving lectures to Peter. I corrected him a thousand times a day in my reasonable and attractive style, nitpicking about posture, and table manners, and grammar, and wearing your clothes right, and God knows what else.

▬

Peter stood on his bike in front of our house. It had twenty-inch wheels, bright red, with seven gears and fancy brakes of the kind that parents cannot repair without spending money. He was half-turned backwards, looking at the rear brake.

"Look, Dad. Something is wrong with the brake when I push it — just watch."

"It's working, Peter. I'm not sure what you mean," and I really was not.

"Why don't you step off the bike," said Betsy. He did. She demonstrated, moving the bike with the handlebar and squeezing the back brake, which locked on the rear wheel exactly as it should.

"But if you squeeze slowly —"

"No, Peter. This happens every year. You play with something on the brakes until they don't work anymore, and then we have to spend money getting them fixed," I said.

"Did you touch something on the brake?" asked Betsy.

"Yes," he admitted, pointing to a rubber sleeve on the brake caliper.

"Push it back to where it was." He pouted, whether over the non-failure of the brake or the matter-of-fact way we were talking to him was hard to say. I supposed that at the symbolic level that damn brake stood for something else that was bothering him, some private pain he couldn't express. Or he was just feeling pissy.

Betsy told him that this year he'd have to pay himself for any brake repairs necessitated by his own fiddling, and I thought about how exhausting it was to have to constantly decide when an action or object was freighted with symbolic meaning and when, *pace* Freud, a brake was just a brake. When to interpret Peter's actions and words in terms of his traumatic background, and when to treat him just like any other nine-year-old kid, was something Betsy and I frequently talked about.

—

One weekend that summer Jeremy and I stood back-to-back and Betsy held a level over our heads to measure our relative heights. I was still marginally taller than him, but he was officially over six feet. He'd become a history major and was working hard in school, and had moved out of his mother's house and begun paying rent.

Upstairs he and the boys played with an elaborate Lego toy that Betsy's father had given them for Christmas, a robot controlled from a computer. We had put the boys on notice that Jeremy was the boss and that he could banish them if they grabbed things or yelled or failed to listen. But Jeremy was patient and firm and the boys listened.

Watching them at the table together, I wondered what I'd learned from being Jeremy's father. The night before, he'd called me in an elated state: he scored in the ninety-fourth percentile on the law school admission test. He knew what he wanted: he was going to law school. It looked like he was finally on track. And however little I'd had to do with that, maybe the fact that I didn't have a fucking clue was somehow OK. My sons were OK.

VII

The ceiling fan in the boys' bedroom needed to be replaced. When you turned it on, the whole fixture shook as if we lived in an earthquake zone. Betsy and I set aside a Friday afternoon when the boys were at daycare.

I hated jobs like this. They affected me like an inquisitorial psychoanalyst, pushing and prodding for my weak spots, frustrating me until I lost control. Doing the job with Betsy especially scared me. She has a talent for spatial relations while I can't even read maps, never mind diagrams for assembling a ceiling fan. The potential for a fight was large, for humiliation almost certain. There was a difference this time, though: Betsy and I promised we'd be patient with each other.

I turned the breaker off in the basement. Removing the old ceiling fan took only about fifteen minutes and involved some satisfying deployment of brute force on my part. But assembling the new fan was a painstaking and slow process that consumed two hours. Betsy read the diagram and found the parts. I turned screws and held bolts in place. Finally we were ready to install. As I held up the new ceiling fan my arms strained and started to tremble. Betsy used the electric drill to turn the last screws in. I could smell my sweat as the afternoon sun climbed through the southern-facing window.

I turned the breaker back on and ran up the stairs to try the fan. No luck. I refused to become impatient, instead driving to the hardware store to buy a cheap circuit tester. Again I held the sixty-pound fixture with my arms pounding as Betsy unscrewed it from the ceiling. The tester showed that there was electricity at the ceiling box. Our connections were secure and clean. Something must be wrong with the fan. I let myself cuss a little and even Betsy declared herself frustrated. We grinned at each other and disassembled the fan just as the boys came home.

I returned the ceiling fan to the hardware store, my third visit in 24 hours, exchanging it for another unit and making sure that this box was factory-sealed. When I got back, Peter and Bohdan were splayed side by side on the front sidewalk, playing with toy cars and trucks. Peter had used a fat yellow chunk of sidewalk chalk to write:

WARNING
Happy Family here
Do Not Enter!

When he saw me he jumped up and opened the door so I could heft the ceiling fan into the house. I called Betsy outside to see Peter's sign.

On Saturday Betsy and I assembled the new fan. This time it took less than an hour and the fixture felt lighter when I held it up. And this time it worked. I gave Betsy a hug and we held each other for a minute, more hugging than we'd done for two years.

VIII

That July we set out for North Carolina to the beach where Betsy had gone as a kid, the trip we'd been planning for almost two years. The weather was hot and by the time we reached Virginia, our fourth day on the road, it was scorching. Like Humbert driving through America in *Lolita*, we looked for the Functional Motel, although our definition was duller than his: we wanted free breakfast, preferably with waffles, a swimming pool, and a predictable level of cleanliness.

Our last motel on the trip south was in Goldsboro, less than a hundred miles from the beach. We stayed in a Super 8 that had free waffles but no pool; we'd be in the ocean the next day anyway.

In the morning as we got dressed, Bohdan heard a scratch at the door. It was a starving orange kitten who cried in a miniature voice. Bohdan fed the kitten some milk from the breakfast room. He and Peter wanted to take it with us. We said no, but Betsy promised she'd call the local humane society to see if they could rescue the kitten.

When we stopped for gas on the way out of Goldsboro, Betsy made the call. A lot of abandoned kittens showed up in the area, the humane society said, and they had too many. Other animal shelters said the same thing. What if the kitten didn't find any food, Peter wanted to know. Maybe someone will adopt it, I said, trying to sound hopeful. Bohdan refused to speak. It was impossible to explain to them that the world is full of orphaned creatures and you cannot rescue them all.

The beach was close enough that we could smell the air changing. Within two hours we arrived on the Crystal Coast of North Carolina, and then crossed the causeway onto Emerald Isle. We picked up the keys to our beach house at the real estate office and drove five more minutes to a section of the island that was so narrow you could see the sound on one side and the Atlantic on the other. We carried our luggage into the house and changed into swimsuits without unpacking. Betsy insisted that we all apply sunscreen. There was a low sand dune just beyond the house and then nothing but ocean. The boys sprinted into the water with their boogie boards. They dove into the waves and splashed each other, hooting and singing.

The sand burned hot under our feet and the sun blazed down. I'd forgotten the buoyancy of salt water and this was the first time I'd swum in the ocean unprotected by a reef. The surf crashed into me, rattling my legs, dropping shells and smooth rocks on the sand. Looking in either direction up the beach I saw miles of white sand and pure blue sky marked only by jet trails. The dunes just off the beach sprouted sea oats and low palms and the water was emerald green or sometimes a translucent blue, depending on the sun's angle.

While Betsy was showing Peter and Bohdan how to body-surf, I headed for the deck to read for an hour. Then I went back to the water with the boys, bodysurfing awkwardly compared to their relaxed movements, and Betsy took her turn on a beach chair. We'd discovered a sandbar just off shore that let us wade in shallow water for a long way. In the late afternoon we took cold showers in the hot sun on the deck, and at night we slept deep and dreamless.

The days passed, indistinct. The first of our two weeks at the beach was done, but it felt like we still had forever. I made only one diary entry and read only one book, the Edith Grossman translation of *Don Quixote*. The boys walked for miles on the beach early in the morning with Betsy, gathering shells and stones, and then maintained strictly proprietary collections in buckets on the deck. Peter began to tan a smooth copper shade, as he always does in a fierce sun, while the rest of us looked pasty and northern.

We fell into a lazy routine. After breakfast we let the boys drink Coke on the beach, something normally off-limits. Then they bodysurfed all morning while either Betsy or I kept an eye on them and the other adult read. After lunch we all piled in the car and went for groceries, or to the county library, or to the aquarium. Stepping out of the car's air-conditioning and into the midday heat was like colliding with a wall pushing us into a drowsy, semi-conscious state.

For bigger grocery trips we went to the Piggly Wiggly in Swansboro on the mainland. I bought T-shirts for Jeremy and for myself that said *I'm Big on the Pig*. We devoted serious attention to snack foods unavailable in Canada such as Flip-Sides — which taste like pretzels on one side and a cracker on the other — and Nutter Butters, a great source of processed peanut butter flavour.

Then we hit the beach again for the afternoon, followed by cocktail hour, during which we enjoyed the gourmet snack foods, more tooth-rotting soda, and incredibly cheap Australian wine for the adults. At the end of cocktail hour a designated parent and child paired up to cook dinner. Bedtime was early for everyone. Betsy and I read the Dave Barry prequels to *Peter Pan* out loud to the boys, or let them watch TV in their bedroom. I checked the weather channel, marvelling how each day promised to be as monotonously perfect as the last. We slept with a fan on, but in spite of her peri-menopause, I put my arm around Betsy for a few minutes after lights out and she snuggled into me.

Toward the start of our second week I was out past the sandbar where the surf ran strong, Bohdan beside me lazing on his boogie board. Betsy and Peter were swimming closer to the beach. In the blinding sunshine about ten yards away, two creatures leapt out of the water, perfectly synchronized, with large fins on their backs. For a moment I panicked, thinking they were sharks. Then I realized they were dolphins and called to Peter and Betsy. They turned around just in time for all four of us to see the dolphins jump once again out of the water together.

—

Every day I'd spend several hours reading *Don Quixote*. It was much funnier and sadder than I recalled from reading it in my twenties. After the sorrowful knight is thrashed by the mule-driver, the narrator says that "he took refuge in his usual remedy, which was to think about some situation from his books," an obvious kind of "madness."

Sitting on the deck chair, with the pulsing heat of the sun on my arms and reflecting off the bright red cover of the novel, I understood why Betsy had seemed so impatient with me since her mother died. When I dived low into a wave alongside Peter and Bohdan, all of us laughing like idiots at the water's force, or when the four of us savoured fresh shrimp fried in butter at dinner, or when I simply held Betsy's hand in the quiet evening, I discovered what she already knew: you have only one life; if it affords you extra chances, that makes you damned lucky, and you'd better jump in and enjoy the ride.

When Betsy and I were on the deck with our books that evening after the boys had gone to bed, my old confidence seemed to come back. I might not be able to distinguish dolphins from sharks, but I did understand my wife. The next day my back hurt but the rest of me sang like Walt Whitman.

On our last Friday it rained for an hour and in the afternoon a rainbow appeared in the northeast, with a purple sky above and a perfect blue below. The ocean darkened in layers, with a thin line of pale blue at the horizon. I stood silently on the rough wood of the deck with the boys and we stared at the sky, at the spray of surf falling like white hair against the greenish waves on the beach. I put my arms around their bony, widening shoulders, and I felt rooted to them and to this spot. There was a certain slant of light on this summer afternoon that made me believe, for a moment, in the eternal.

BACK IN THE USSR

We returned from North Carolina to an early fall, the season when trees shed their leaves and the cold sets in, when you remember things, as Peter told me two years ago, with your body — dark, hidden things you would rather not know.

The boys returned to school, and Betsy to work, and I returned to my study and took up some notes I'd made about my grandfather back in 2003. I had come to a dead end. There were no official records other than his death certificate, and no witnesses had survived. For raw material I had interviewed my surviving uncles who had been in Soviet prisons, and read Solzhenitsyn's *Gulag Archipelago* more than once. Now I stared at the computer screen until it became invisible, and a ghostly feeling came into my fingers as I felt my way back to what his last chapter must have been like.

The Black Maria skulked like a short hearse, parked in front of my grandfather's house in Nikolaifeld, Ukraine. It was late December 1937, the middle of the night. My dad was two months old.

Four men exited the Black Maria and knocked hard on the door. They had come for my dad's father, Cornelius Mierau. Two of the men were teenagers carrying rifles with fixed bayonets. The others were men from the village who helped the communists round up troublemakers in exchange for immunity from persecution.

Lil remembered: the white lace tablecloth in the kitchen, the dirty boots of the men who came for her dad, and how rusty the bayonets on the rifles looked in the candlelight. She remembered her father hoisting her up on his shoulders for one last ride while the men with the rifles waited, looking down at their dirty boots. She was five years old and her father was thirty-six.

My father was asleep in the crib while his mother cried, pleaded, moaned, until the noise of her terror woke him and he cried too. The Black Maria drove away with Cornelius.

——

Cornelius loved music. He built stringed instruments, and he could play violin, seven-string guitar, mandolin, flute, piano. In jail, without any instruments except his voice, he hummed quietly to himself. The guard told him to shut up. In the silence he could not escape memories of Lil's soft dark hair when he touched her head the last time, his son's smooth arms and milky burps, Helen's beautiful forehead, the proud way she held it up even though they were poor. Would he ever lie in bed with her again, smell her nightclothes? He tried to clear his mind by repeating a prayer, over and over again.

Early the next morning the men drove Cornelius thirty kilometres to the city of Zaporozhye, where the GPU, Stalin's secret police, used the local prison's basement for interrogations. The basement was useful because it had many small rooms with thin walls, so the sounds prisoners made travelled easily to the other rooms and even outside, where wives and families could hear and were meant to hear.

Cornelius was accused of treason under Section 58 of the penal code for refusing to sing a communist song with his youth group, and for poisoning some farm horses. The charges themselves didn't matter. There was a quota of German nationals from this area who had to die.

One of the GPU guards led Cornelius into a room with boarded-up windows. The guard grabbed Cornelius's collar and spun him like a top, before throwing him to the floor. Cornelius was light, small to begin with and undernourished. As he fell, he hit a chair. He heard his ribs cracking and he slumped into the corner clutching his chest. He stayed there all night, trying to picture himself at home, or in church, playing a high note on the violin as a harmonic, his imagined touch on the string transcending the pain that staggered him.

"Toilet?" said the guard next morning, waking him up from where he lay crumpled on the floor.

"Yes, toilet," he said, and he was taken to a little shed behind the building. The door had been removed. There was no water or toilet paper. He got shit on his shoes but there was no time to wipe it off.

The guard hustled Cornelius back into his cell. He saw no one except when he was given a meal or taken to the toilet. From the other cells he heard shouts, slaps, thuds, and almost every day, gunshots from the yard above. He tried to remember musical scores, hymns, the bass lines on a seven-string guitar. He moved his hands as if playing a guitar, or touching his children's hair. He would spend more than a month like this, waiting.

One early morning Cornelius was taken from his cell to the interrogation team, always a troika who voted on the prisoner's fate. The three men stood around a table with a single piece of paper on it.

"This is your confession. Read and sign." The leader was a

ruddy, tall man with highly polished black boots who held his back stiffly erect. He sniffed the air as if the smell of it bothered him. The troika leader reminded Cornelius of a deacon in their church, an officious man who dressed carefully and made deals with the bosses. The leader's second placed a pistol on the table. Out of the corner of his eye, Cornelius could see a large bloodstain on the wall at head level.

"These are lies," said Cornelius. One of the troika moved suddenly and pistol-whipped him. Cornelius saw blood drip from his head onto the table. The pain was outside him now, his vision fuzzy. He imagined the communion wine in church, how it stained your fingers when it spilled over the cup's edge.

"I won't sign," said Cornelius, knowing this was not about justice, that they didn't care if he signed the paper. "What will you do with me?" No one answered him. He thought of Jesus on the cross, beaten and calling to his father, but that was sacrilege. He was not Jesus. He calculated the odds of his own survival. They were not good.

Prisoners who did not sign confessions were shot immediately because there was no way to transport all of them to Siberia. The Stolypin train cars held only thirty-five people even if prisoners were stacked like salamanders, and there was little to feed them once they arrived at Construction Project 501, the tundra-spanning railroad in northern Siberia. In addition, there was always the quota to consider, and unreformable political prisoners like Cornelius were perfect for filling it.

Two guards grabbed him by the shoulders of his coat. He heard it tear. They pushed him against the wall near the bloodstain. He pulled his mind away and saw the fresh dill cut into soup, white potato slice, red beet floating in broth, the callous on his wife's thumb where she gripped the knife. One of the guards held a gun to his head. The other held up the paper with the charges.

"I won't sign," Cornelius said. His bowels gave way and he smelled the shit just as he heard the explosion like a string snapping on one of his violins, the f-hole near his head, and brains and bone fragments spattered on the wall, enlarging the stain.

"Get a goddamn bucket," said one of the guards. "Regier will kill us if this place stinks any worse. Next time shoot at the neck and do it outside."

My grandmother Helen tried to visit Cornelius in Zaporozhye. She took food for her husband, *zwieback*, dried prunes, and wool long underwear to keep him warm in Siberia, hoping they had not sent him away already, that he was still alive. Gunshots often rang out, but she'd heard that only the criminals got killed. Her husband was not a criminal. When she reached the front of the line, they took her food and promised to give it to Cornelius Mierau. She walked home without a glimpse of him and returned with food once a week for four weeks. Prisoners' wives could only come on Sundays.

In early February, she met with Cornelius's best friend, Gerhard Bergen. He'd been arrested with Cornelius, and also accused of being an enemy of the state. The charge against Gerhard was singing religious songs and strangling piglets on the collective farm. He'd seen Cornelius taken into a small room and heard the gunshot. Gerhard signed his own confession immediately, expecting to get at least ten years in a labour camp, if he survived at all. Instead they released him right away. There were shortages of bullets and so he was lucky.

"Helen, don't wait for Cornelius," he said.

"Do you know if he signed a confession?"

"He never did."

I stopped typing. Somehow the act of imagining my grandfather's horrific death, the brutality of his end, had laid something to rest in me. I sent a copy to my father and he had nothing to say about it. But his silence no longer frustrated me. Dad didn't want this shit on his mind. I didn't either. Now that the words lay like black grave markers on the white paper, I could leave the museum of the past.

CUBA

For spring break in 2011 I planned to make my yearly visit to Edmonton with the boys, and in mid-March I called Dad to make arrangements.

"Have you watched the Lakers since the All-Star Game?" he said, after we exchanged greetings.

"Yeah. They're struggling to win with Kobe Bryant back in the lineup. Shouldn't happen to such a good team."

"Well, Kobe doesn't pass, right? You said it yourself last time."

"True enough. So are we OK for spring break? I'm hoping to get to your place by midday on Sunday."

"Well," he hedged, "your sister's really busy leading all her choirs, and I'm helping her of course. Your mother gets worried with extra noise and people — and I've been seeing a doctor."

"Why didn't you tell me sooner? I wish we'd known." I knew that my mother's "worry" was my father's euphemism for her worsening dementia, but it was unusual for Dad to see a doctor, and I was concerned. I sent an email to my sister, who said she really was too busy to handle guests. My mother was much worse too, she said, and Dad was on blood-thinners.

My father's refusal to plan ahead was nothing new — as a kid I often didn't know what country we'd be in the next year — but still I was upset that he'd left it so late to cancel our trip.

I felt the old anger flare. Here was my father once again affecting all our lives on the spur of the moment: the boys who were looking forward to the visit, Betsy who enjoyed her week away from us, and me, left to figure out how to spend spring break without disappointing everyone.

But as Betsy pointed out, I needed more to connect with my sons than with my father, and she suggested we go to Cuba for spring break. We spent a single frantic night on the Internet looking at all-inclusive vacation prices and customer reviews, and pictures of women with girlish thighs on extremely white beaches. It turned out that my father's procrastination had paid off in one way: a profusion of great last-minute specials.

Unfortunately, like one of those saboteurs Stalin and his henchmen constantly invented, Peter tended to undercut the state, especially when the state delivered good things. So the day before we left for Cuba Peter had a bad day in school, talking out of turn, wandering around the classroom when he was supposed to sit, shoving a classmate on the stairs. And the day we were to leave, Peter woke up after terrible dreams. He had dreamed that he was in a room in Ukraine with his family. He couldn't see their bodies, only their heads, and when he reached toward them, to touch them, he realized they were faceless, and then they disappeared completely.

At breakfast Peter wanted to talk about his birth family, not the trip to Cuba, even though his whole body vibrated with trip-related tension. "How come we don't know anything about my family?" he demanded.

"We do know some things, and we've told you everything we know," I said. "We know the names of your grandparents, and also exactly what village you were born in, and what part of western Ukraine near Poland your family lived in. Keep eating your cereal, Peter. They were likely there for centuries, farming the land when it was owned by Polish nobility."

"But there are no pictures of my mother or my father."

"That's true."

"If you were my father you could tell me more about my family." He said this in a neutral tone, with his mouth full of cereal, and I was not offended.

"You're right. But I'll tell you something. My family tree on your grandpa's side, from when they lived in Ukraine, with the names of uncles and aunts and their children, it's not complete either. My family was poor on both Grandpa and Grandma's sides and they didn't keep proper records. And you know what else happened?"

"What?"

"War. When there's armies and destruction, people have to run away and they often lose important documents, pictures, diaries, all kinds of things that matter to the family." I told him about how embarrassment over poor spelling had prevented my family members from writing down what happened to the Mierau great-grandparents. I didn't tell him that maybe they failed to write the truth because it was just so awful.

"Take those vitamins, buddy. You too, Bohdan. We have to finish packing."

—

We landed in Camaguey, on Cuba's north shore, at about midnight, with Peter and Bohdan still wide awake. Walking across the tarmac of the small airport I could feel the tropical humidity envelop my body like a nostalgic wave. I'd told the boys how beautiful the beaches were in Jamaica when I lived there as a boy. They were punch-drunk with exhaustion, clinging to my hands as we got in line for our tourist visas.

An hour later we slouched in the back of a Chinese-made bus driving to our resort. The boys still had not slept, and their eyes rolled around in their heads with every jolt on the narrow, pockmarked road. Someone at the front announced that the air-conditioning couldn't run or else the driver's window would fog up. I tried to follow the logic of this but my brain had stopped functioning.

About half an hour from the resort all three of us fell asleep. When the bumps and rolls stopped we woke up grouchy and disoriented. The resort's lobby had no outer walls and we stood in line in the sea breeze for twenty minutes to check in. The bellman led us through a labyrinth of sidewalks past the pool, the buffet restaurant, various low buildings, until we reached our room. He stood in the doorway after showing me the controls for the air conditioner and I tipped him five Canadian dollars since there had been no chance to get local currency yet.

The room was crowded with the three beds I requested and no chest of drawers was visible. But the air conditioner worked fine. It was past two in the morning and we fell into bed in our underwear without brushing teeth or unpacking.

The morning sun penetrated the room's curtains and woke us up by seven. I opened the closet and found a pressboard chest of drawers that had been stuffed inside to create floor space for our three beds. The room was clean and bare with high ceilings and tropical light coming in through the French doors.

I got the boys up and we unpacked. Then I called a family meeting even though every fibre of my jangled, sleep-deprived brain wanted to get coffee as absolutely soon as possible.

"We're going to have breakfast now at the buffet. I need you guys to stay with me. Peter, can you please look at me?" Peter was fidgeting and reaching around me for the TV remote, completely distracted.

"Yes, Dad."

"You're still not making eye contact."

"DAD I'M HUNGRY," shouted Bohdan.

"OK, let's go."

Outside the sky was azure blue and the sun touched your skin like a masseuse. I retraced the bellman's steps from last night and we found the pool and buffet. The boys ran off to investigate the food and the room. Peter had near-crashes with several guests and I decided to just get my coffee and ignore it.

We regrouped at a table near the lineup for breakfast. Peter loaded up on fruit and bread. Bohdan and I got omelettes with bacon on the side. The breakfast chef wore a white hat and smock, and sported a sly smile. For the next seven days he would be there every morning, remembering that I liked a three-egg omelette with cheese, green peppers, onions, ham.

After breakfast Peter wanted to explore the resort on his own. I relented because it was small and the staff helpful and friendly. Bohdan and I went to the beach where the sand was miraculously white and fine on your feet, the sun hot without blistering, and later that day, the water warm behind a coral reef. Under an umbrella I read a Gary Shteyngart novel on a borrowed Kindle, which I carried everywhere inside a beach towel to keep it dry.

The boys and I rented a pedal boat and Peter refused to let anyone else steer. When I insisted that we all take turns, he jumped off the boat and tried pulling it in the opposite direction. While Peter and I argued, Bohdan got off the boat into the shallow water and played with a starfish an Italian man gave him.

I gave up and left Peter the pedal boat. The boys started fighting as soon as Bohdan tried to board, their yells echoing down the beach. I put Peter in a time-out since he refused to share. He glared at me murderously.

A spirit of irritation filled me like a bone-weariness and I thought, *I am too old for this shit*. In a parallel universe I could have been here with a different wife, without kids, without responsibility. But Peter's beautiful, emphatically determined face was the image of my dilemma: I could not imagine being without him. His stubborn, joyous enthusiasm and dark anger resembled my own. But he was not an extension of my personality or my family history. He bore my name, but he was entirely himself.

━━

Late in the morning all the guests who'd travelled with the same charter company met with a sales rep. She was chatty, round, relaxed, getting along in English, French, and Italian. She told me her grandparents had come to Cuba from Jamaica looking for work in the 1940s. Her grandfather cut sugar cane. I said that I'd lived in Jamaica as a boy and felt tempted to chat a bit more, but after the small talk, she was all business. I bought several excursions: a tour of a crocodile refuge and a violin factory, a snorkelling trip out at the big Atlantic reef, and a tour of historic Camaguey, a UNESCO world heritage site.

After lunch at the buffet we went for a swim in the pool. What most enthralled the boys was the swim-up bar where they could get unlimited soft drinks. It occupied them all afternoon. I sipped watery Cuban beer at the bar and read a novel while Peter and Bohdan experienced several hours of sugar high, running amok around the pool.

The next morning I took a two-mile run while the boys lolled in bed and watched TV. The resort was on a barren service road that connected a gas station, a nightclub, and several other resorts. Mangrove swamp grew on the road's other side, and the sidewalk past the resort cracked and heaved.

In the parking lot I met Julio, who had a horse and carriage and offered to give me a tour of the nearby village. I promised to come back with my sons later in the morning. I wanted them to see how people lived here, how not everyone goes on a holiday where they get endless beverage refills.

I insisted the boys have a shower, and we started our carriage tour just before noon, wearing hats and greased up with sunscreen. Julio began by taking us outside the "Zona Turistica" to the narrow highway we'd driven from the airport.

Bohdan sat up front with Julio. He fidgeted and removed his hat. Julio turned to me. "Tropicale uh," and he pointed at the sun.

"You have to wear your hat, Bohdan." Bohdan replaced his hat but dropped his spending money on the road. Julio stopped the carriage and we scoured the road and the short grass at the edge. No success. Bohdan knew I wouldn't replace it and he pouted until the horse relieved himself on the road, which distracted him.

In the village we saw a bright yellow apartment block just off the main road. Peter wanted to know why laundry hung from the windows. I explained that they could use the sun to dry their clothes, since it was nearly always warm.

We drove past rows of tiny one-storey houses made of brick with tin roofs. Dogs and cats swarmed the roads and yards.

"Why are the dogs so skinny? Don't they feed them?"

"People here are poor, Bohdan. The dogs probably just get scraps from the kitchen."

"When I grow up I'd like to come back and give everyone some money," said Peter.

"I'll come back and feed the animals," said Bohdan.

—

The next morning after breakfast we went to the crocodile farm. On the bus the tour guide told us that Cuba had two kinds of mangrove, red and green. Oddly the red mangrove clumped on one side of the road, the green on the other, as if making a statement about racial purity. Drinking water had to be piped in from a distance to this swampy area because the local water was too salty.

We passed ranches and the guide pointed out the white, golden-billed egrets in the fields with Cuban cattle. We stopped at a flea market of Chinese-made goods laid out on a town square's sidewalk. The square was clean but the paint peeled off the buildings in grey flakes. The only new vehicles were Chinese, and all the others looked like a vintage American automobile show.

Our next stop was a violin factory, a one-storey structure like a barn, painted white. It smelled pleasantly of sawdust and sweat. All the workers were male, ranging from boys to old men. The guide said they made violins and guitars out of native wood and Canadian maple when available, only for Cuban schools, not for export, though of course they would sell to the tourists. Bohdan depleted his remaining spending money to buy a toy drum and Peter got a miniature guitar.

The boys were quiet at the crocodile farm. Neither of them touched the baby croc held up for a group of kids, and they both jumped backwards when a giant croc had to be restrained with a pole. As hundreds of crocs competed for food in the red mud, Bohdan said he was scared because "they can bite your hands off."

A couple of days later we went snorkelling on the outer reef, one of Papa Hemingway's old haunts. We took a bus to the dock and waited for our yacht. The boat to the reef was crowded with tourists wearing lifejackets. Peter and Bohdan were the only kids and they wanted to sit on the front of the yacht, in the open, and I said no because it was too easy to fall off. But I gave in after ten minutes of pleading, even though it meant we had to walk on a six-inch strip of metal to the front deck, with only a delicate railing to hold.

The wind blew hard and I panicked every time the boys repositioned themselves on the smooth white deck, but they were enraptured with the sensation of the boat bouncing on the waves and the wind whipping salt into our faces.

As we neared the reef an older retired man, a Canadian, said to me that my boys were at a great age, a time when you could really enjoy them. I nodded agreeably and wondered why worry kept interfering with my pleasure in their eagerness and enthusiasm.

The boat stopped and we all put on masks, snorkels, and fins. The water was warm and clear, teeming with fish. The coral looked like a work of art, as if God had worked out fractals on a computer he built with his own gnarled, hairy white hands. I noticed Peter swimming in the opposite direction from everyone else and nudged him back to the group. He nodded so vigorously that his snorkel dipped underwater and he came up spitting water, then he followed me without any drama.

—

Bohdan had become obsessed with the stray cats that haunted the resort, and one in particular who was starving and pregnant. "Why don't they fix the cats so they don't have kittens?" he asked, and I explained they probably didn't have money for that. We were eating lunch at a grill that made burgers, fries, hot dogs. The starving cat twined through Bohdan's legs.

"Get her a chicken burger, just the meat," I said to him. He was back in ten minutes and put the meat on the flagstone floor. I'd never seen a cat eat so quickly and indelicately. Bohdan smiled continuously while the cat bolted down the burger patty.

Then Bohdan ran off to the pool, looking for Peter. I followed at a leisurely pace, ready for the courtly politeness of the bartenders.

—

"I saw a boy playing with one of the cats today," Bohdan said at dinner that night, "and he wasn't wearing shoes."

Peter raised his eyebrows as if about to contradict him.

"You know, when we lived in Jamaica," I said, "some of the kids went without shoes. Their families were poor, and they only wore shoes on Sunday to church."

"Doesn't that hurt your feet?" asked Peter.

"Yes, but you get callouses so you don't feel it much. Still, I was like you guys. I wished that I could give everyone money so they would have shoes like mine."

"Were you rich?" asked Bohdan.

"No, not at all. But we had a lot of money compared to the other kids' families. My sister and I were the only white students out of 500 in the school. Sometimes the kids would pinch our skin to see what it would look like."

"That's not nice," said Bohdan.

"They didn't mean to hurt us." I took a drink of thin Cuban beer and a deep breath. "But I was like you guys are in school. I felt very lonely there."

"But you had your mom and dad," Bohdan said.

"Yes, I did," I said, not bothering to point out that he had parents too. It wasn't the same.

—

Horses often grazed by the resort's outer fence and one day I agreed we could go see them for a few minutes, but no petting. Suddenly a large iguana lurched past the fence, stopped short at the sight of us, and waddled toward the shrubbery. Bohdan no longer cared about horses — he sprinted after the iguana and grabbed him by the middle before I could do more than sputter *Let go, let go!* I was terrified and frozen in place. The iguana was almost the size of Bohdan and had nasty-looking claws on his back feet, which rotated in the air like an upended truck. Bohdan let go and the iguana sprinted away from him on its comically short legs, likely more frightened than Bohdan, who ambled back to us.

That night we made our usual phone call to Betsy. She told us how much she loved us, how much work she'd gotten done, how she'd washed the floors, how Peter should try not to argue with me and his brother, how Bohdan should listen and be polite, and how I shouldn't stress out too much about Bohdan losing the power supply for his Nintendo DS. I did not tell her that an iguana almost killed Bohdan. We signed off, brushed teeth, and went to bed.

▬

On our last night I told the boys they could spend an hour watching cartoons on TV in our room while I went out. The only cartoons were in Spanish but that didn't bother them. Peter even claimed to understand bits of the dialogue, which was possible: he'd spent four years in French immersion classrooms.

"Where are you going?" said Bohdan.

"I want to buy cigars for one of my friends."

Peter shook his head.

"Can't you die from smoking?" Bohdan asked, a reasonable question. Freud died from smoking twenty cigars a day. Fidel still hung on.

"Not if you don't smoke very often." This was a grey area and I left quickly, heading out of the resort to the nearby gas station, which I knew was open in the evening. They sold only cigarettes.

"Amour, amore," sang out a pair of modestly dressed young prostitutes. At night the hookers congregated on the available benches along the broken-down road, wearing eye-watering perfume.

"No, gracias."

A rail-thin woman with old eyes and a bright red dress approached me and grabbed my hand.

I shook her off and said, "I'm only looking for cigars."

"You want box, I have a friend. Twenty-five dollars."

"No, I only want a few."

"You on vacacione, heh," she leered, exposing several missing teeth, and struggling to keep up with me. "Sucky sucky, fucky fucky, sex on the beach, twenty pesos."

"No, gracias señora." Repulsed and wanting to get rid of her, I gave her a couple of pesos, probably enough to buy a hand job. A gaudily dressed man had followed close behind her, likely a pimp, which put him in the same job often filled by the most enterprising and aggressive former orphanage boys in Ukraine. I looked at my watch and began running back to the resort. I should never have come out there.

Back in our room I kissed the boys on their foreheads and they both did a double take at my unusual display of affection.

The next morning I solved my cigar problem in the simplest possible way, by buying three premium cigars at the tobacco store in the resort. The package had a barcode and a government seal.

—

We said goodbye to the beach and the pool, and Peter cried silently. After dinner I cut the boys off soft drinks and we checked out of our room, leaving our luggage in the lobby. Our checkout time left us six hours to kill before the airport bus arrived. Keeping the boys awake and cheerful would be difficult.

Our flight home was the red-eye. Peter read and dozed, Bohdan watched a *Shrek* sequel and, after trying unsuccessfully to read, I watched *Unstoppable*, in which Denzel Washington prevents an apocalyptic train crash. Despite the formulaic setup, and probably because of my exhaustion, I found myself filled with weepy longing for Denzel's heroic fatherhood, his tender, uncomplicated relationship with his children, two daughters who worked at Hooters and worshipped him. Denzel wasted no time thinking about the past — he jumped from a speeding train to a speeding truck and back again, saving innocent lives every few seconds. He was handsome cardboard with no messy past. He was the anti-Hamlet. And still I wept.

Bohdan held off sleep until the last credits rolled on his movie just before sunrise. Then he removed his headphones and asked me to wake him up for breakfast. I solemnly promised. He fell immediately into a trance-like sleep.

When Peter set aside his book and fell into deep sleep too, I stared at him for a while, unused to seeing his body in stasis, his face untroubled as water behind a reef. Peter's constant vulnerability wore me out even though my skin rivalled his for thinness, because I wanted him to know that just having genitals that hang outside your body makes you vulnerable enough, without opening yourself any further, without a lot of damn talking. Still asleep, Peter leaned into me hard with his bony shoulder and I put my arm around him and kissed his forehead for the second time in twenty-four hours. Fatherhood was not a single day's rescue mission. Everything Denzel's movie hero knew about being a father was bullshit. Everything I knew about being a father was bullshit too. It didn't matter. I wanted a clean page and an open heart for my sons.

HOME AGAIN

Peter squatted on our front yard cocking a hammer above the sidewalk. On the concrete lay a twisted piece of metal, a computer hard disk. Three more hard disks splayed out from his legs. The computer parts came from Betsy's brother in Illinois, who stipulated that the drives must be destroyed; they were filled with the digital dregs of confidential information.

Peter brought the hammer down on one disk after another, as hard as he could. Tiny machine screws and bits of green circuit board flew into the air around him until he got through the metal casing and began smashing the actual disk. That was where the computer's memory lived, I'd told him, in magnetized bits and bytes on that polished orb.

"Look Dad," he said, "I'm erasing the memory!"

He moved the hammer over to the other drives and soon more fragments of plastic and metal whirred in the air like mechanical hummingbirds. Peter laughed in delight.

On the sidewalk in front of our house Bohdan took exaggerated steps while clutching a black plastic ninja sword in each hand. With each pose he gave a bloodcurdling tae kwon do howl.

I was on the porch watching them, ignoring the book in my hands, a scholarly edition of Milton's *Paradise Regained*, which I'd wanted to read out of some notion of literary self-improvement.

Peter's hammer pulverized another hard disk. I didn't give a damn about Milton's getting paradise back. *Paradise Lost* has always excited me more, the fall into pain and lust and death, the impossibility of justifying God's unattractive ways. I scanned the opening lines just as my youngest son climbed onto my lap:

I, who erewhile the happy Garden sung,
By one man's disobedience lost, now sing
Recovered Paradise to all mankind....

Bohdan interrupted my reading when he plunked himself down. His butt was the boniest, sharpest, most uncomfortable in the world. Peter dropped his hammer and ran toward us, gesturing at the street, and I closed the book. We all waved to Betsy. She smiled at us as she walked home in her long strides from the bus stop.

ACKNOWLEDGEMENTS

Much gratitude to my wife, Elizabeth Troutt. Words fail. Thank you to my sons, Jeremy Clemens-Mierau, Peter Mierau, and Bohdan Mierau, who've tolerated the intrusion of this book into their lives. And thanks to: my parents, Eric and Velma Mierau, for answering my nosy questions and even, perhaps foolishly, lending me their diaries; my aunt Lil Bargen for telling me about the war and her early life with such candour and eloquence; my great-uncle Dietrich (Dick) Wiebe for telling me about the family's escape from East Germany; my great-uncle the late Heinrich (Henry) Wiebe for trying — and failing — to tell me his story.

I must thank my friends and colleagues who read this book in manuscript, sometimes before anyone should have seen it: Jim Anderson, David Bergen, Sandra Birdsell, Nicole Boudreau, Warren Cariou, Chad Colburn, Victor Enns, Heidi Harms, Sally Ito, Carl Matheson, Shane Neilson, Merrell-Ann Phare, John K. Samson, Gregg Shilliday, Melissa Steele, and Joan Thomas (who read it twice and never let me give up).

Institutional support for this project came from the Banff Centre's Writing Studio, the Canada Council, the Manitoba Arts Council, and the Winnipeg Arts Council. At Banff, Michael Crummey and Daphne Marlatt were enormously helpful.

Pages 55–58 of this book appeared in *Rhubarb* magazine in an earlier version. The poem "Soldiers" on p. 116 was published in my book *Ending with Music* (Brick, 2002).

Timothy Snyder's *Bloodlands: Europe Between Hitler and Stalin* (Basic Books, 2010) gave me nightmares and context. Some details in the section "Back in the USSR" come from Aleksandr Solzhenitsyn's *The Gulag Archipelago, 1918–1956*, translated by Thomas P. Whitney (Harper & Row, 1973), and also from Anne Applebaum's chapter on the Great Terror in her book *Gulag: A History* (Doubleday, 2003). The lines from Fernando Pessoa's "Autopsychography" in the opening section are from *Fernando Pessoa & Co.*, edited and translated by Richard Zenith, Grove/Atlantic, 1998.

Thank you to Barbara Scott, an amazing editor. All the errors, distortions, and assorted failures are mine. Thanks as well to Kelsey Attard at Freehand, who makes everything happen.

MAURICE MIERAU is the author of several books of poetry, including *Fear Not,* which won the ReLit Award in 2009. He was born in Indiana, and grew up in Nigeria, Manitoba, Jamaica, Kansas, and Saskatchewan. He now lives in Winnipeg with his family.